Contents

Study Guide of the Archetypes

By Renn Butler

OpenUniverse

www.rennbutler.com

ISBN: 9798843288655

Printed in the United States of America

Preface

Welcome to my class in archetypal and holotropic astrology! I greatly look forward to sharing this quality time together as a group.

This guide is designed to help students in my classes and other students to learn the most important principles of archetypal astrology. The heart of this field is a focus on aspects, transits, and world transits, involving the planetary pairs, from Sun-Moon out to Neptune-Pluto. I wrote this manual to help people stay organized and focus their attention evenly across all these major areas. This book will help you to learn this material in a broad and comprehensive way, maintain your knowledge, and expand your studies going forward.

It is great to have you in the class and I hope you get everything out of this learning experience that you need and hope for.

Study Guide of the Archetypes

If astrology is to evolve, we must get beyond the crude, exoteric, fortune-telling orientation inherited from the past and begin to come to terms with the symbols in a new kind of way. We must learn to feel the symbolism and not merely relate to its surface. . . . In fact, we must become possessed by them, much the way the ancients were by their gods. This is not a call for all astrologers to become insane in order to understand truly what they are about, but more dangerous journeys in life and understanding are called for than most students of astrology have undergone.

Robert Hand (Moon semisextile Mercury, with Moon square Pluto)
"The Moon, the Four Phases of the Feminine," *Essays on Astrology*, 1982

I

Course Format and Resources for Further Learning

Course Format

The new course will begin on September 30, 2023 with classes running from Noon-2:20 pm Pacific time. There will be a ten-minute break at 1 pm.

All classes are recorded, so you do not have to show up live each week and some people cannot come live at all. The people who do come for the majority of classes, however, will tend to get more out of the experience emotionally, but it is totally your choice.

The development of a supportive online community is an important part of this class for many students. After turning off the recording at 2:20, I will keep the Zoom meeting going, and invite anyone who wants to stay longer, to chat and share with each other. These after-class discussions and connections with other students greatly enrich some people's experience of the course, but they are of course optional.

Note: We will be taking December off for Christmas and two or three weeks in March for spring break. We may also take breaks on another Saturday or possibly two. The final class will be at the end of April or the first Saturday in May.

The first half of each class will be devoted to reviewing two or more of the planetary pairs (eg. Sun-Neptune and Moon-Neptune) and I will present a shortened version of my slideshow for each. Students will then have an opportunity to share insights about their charts, and hear those of others, in small breakout sessions. The second half of classes will be devoted to special topics, including explorations of current events, dreams, relationships, and psychedelic session charts. If you have an unusually rich and interesting dream or psychedelic session, please send the writeup to me, with the date of the dream or session. We will look at some of each. I will also demonstrate a number of times how I do natal and transit readings.

What to Expect

In this course we will explore deeply the meanings and effects of the forty-five combinations of planetary archetypes known as the *planetary pairs*—from Sun-Moon out to Neptune-Pluto. Through my slideshows (both sent in advance and reviewed in each class), I will present many rich examples of how these archetypes manifest in the realms of everyday life, dreams, relationship issues, holotropic and psychedelic sessions, literature, philosophy, art, music, film, history, and current events.

We will review Tarnas' correlations of the four outer planets with Grof's perinatal sequence, and their many inflections and variations. You will learn how to use archetypal astrology to choose good days for healing journeys, understand their content, and integrate them afterward. We will talk about the benefits of undergoing deep self-exploration, on both a personal level and for the collective psyche of humanity. Related areas will be the role of the journeyer's inner healer, benefit of evocative music, the role of sitters, and how they can best support the journeyer's unfolding inner process.

One of the most important purposes of astrology is to encourage us to embark on the process of self-exploration, what Joseph Campbell called the Hero or Heroine's Journey. This course will give you greater insight into your unfolding psychospiritual journey and those of the people around you. Pursuing this work in a systematic and responsible way works to clear out the finite pool of negative material in the individual psyche. This automatically opens or widens the pathway to numinous states of Divine Consciousness, beyond death and mortality—experiences which are known to have a meta-healing value in our psyches.

Recommended Reading
(especially *The Archetypal Universe, Pathways to Wholeness,* and
Planets in Transit)

The Archetypal Universe - Renn
Pathways to Wholeness - Renn
The Astrology of Love and Relationships - Renn
    (here is a link to mine: https://www.rennbutler.com/reader-comments)
Prometheus the Awakener - Richard Tarnas
Planets in Transit - Robert Hand
Making the Gods Work for You - Caroline Casey
Horoscope Symbols - Robert Hand
The Way of the Psychonaut - Stan Grof
The Adventure of Self-Discovery - Stan Grof
Cosmos and Psyche - Richard Tarnas
Liz Greene - anything she has written
When the Impossible Happens - Stan Grof
The Archetypal Cosmos - Keiron LeGrice
The Astrology of Human Relationships - Sakoian and Acker
The Astrologer's Handbook - Sakoian and Acker
Planets in Composite - Robert Hand
The Stormy Search for the Self - Stan and Christina Grof

Resources for Further Learning

Archetypal News Network (ANN)
I created this YouTube channel with James Moran and other colleagues in early 2022, and it has become a rich source of informative and entertaining content. Major contributors include Alexis Angelucci, Art Granoff, Alex Stein, and Tatiana Hassan, with offerings by Richard Tarnas, Barbara Yuruvich, Becca Tarnas, Chad Harris, Chris McNulty, Christina Hardy, Danielle Meyer, Dulcie Cardinal, Erica Jones, Lisa Leombruni, Mychal A. Bryan, Rebecca Farrar, Safron Rossi, and others.

Class Facebook Group
Be sure to subscribe to our class Facebook group. (I sent you the link in the class welcome letter.) It is not essential to join but will add some additional interactive elements to the class.

Archetypal Astrology and Transpersonal Psychology Group on Facebook
A good resource for ongoing posts and information in this field.

Richard Tarnas' Article, "Introduction to Archetypal Astrology"
This is a brilliant and classic introduction to archetypal astrology and the planetary archetypes, which became the opening chapters of *Cosmos and Psyche*.
www.archetypalnews.net/resources

Online and Recorded Archetypal Astrology Courses by Colleagues
James Moran is offering live and prerecorded classes, which integrate Grof and Tarnas' work—sharing the same understandings and perspectives of my own.
www.jamesmoran.org

Becca Tarnas' recorded course "Awakening to Archetypal Astrology"
www.academyoforaclearts.mykajabi.com/Awakening%20to%20Archetypal%20Astrology

Art Granoff is also offering online courses which integrate the Grof-Tarnas perspective.
www.referenceastrology.com
I highly recommend all of their classes.

Becca Tarnas' Study Guide
I will email this to you in September.

Art Granoff's Voice Recordings of my book, *The Archetypal Universe*
www.soundcloud.com/user-648408384

Important Graphics
The Grof-Tarnas Perinatal Sequence, the COEX Graphic, and Lisa Leombruni's Orb Table. I will email these to you in early October.

Archetypal Explorer Program
This acclaimed program created by Kyle Nicholas has many brilliant features and innovations. Accessible and easy to use, I recommend it highly for both students and professionals in the field of astrology. Available for a free trial period.
www.archetypalexplorer.com

Kyle Pierce's *Planetdance* Program
This interesting and innovative new program created by Kyle Pierce accesses the entire database of Wikipedia biographies. You can also do searches for multiple aspects at once. These features will enable quantum leaps in new correlations research.
www.jcremers.com (check out the Coincidings app on the menu)
And Kyle's blog about the program: symbolistics.wordpress.com

"Archai: The Journal of Archetypal Cosmology"
An academic journal that explores significant correlations between cyclical alignments of the planets and the archetypal patterns of human experience.
www.archai.org

A Different Doorway: Adventures of a Caesarean Born by Jane English
www.eheart.com/cesareanvoices/DD-revised.pdf

Astrotheme
A comprehensive online database of famous people's charts, for quick searches.
www.astrotheme.com

Astrodienst
A good site for casting a chart quickly, if you don't have your own program.
www.astro.com

Solar Fire Program
I use and love this program. The Mac version is Astro Gold.

Changing of the Gods
The evocative and captivating documentary about the Uranus-Pluto cycle in history—including the recent square of 2007-2021—is based on Richard Tarnas' *Cosmos and Psyche*.
www.changingofthegods.com

The Way of the Psychonaut
Susan Hess Logeais' brilliant documentary about the profound lifework and thera-peutic discoveries of Stanislav Grof, M.D.
www.thewayofthepsychonaut.com

Music for Holotropic and Psychedelic Sessions
1) Johns Hopkins' sets for psilocybin therapy sessions on Spotify:
https://open.spotify.com/playlist/5KWf8H2pM0tlVd7niMtqeU

2) Breathwork sets (about three hours each) on Spotify created by Riley Thomson Smith:
a)https://open.spotify.com/playlist/5sAYbQlSuBd3GVrW4xeuQs?fbclid=I
wAR3yagtipIDQBqSf5VJ15C1LmUKYW_YZObmgqx4ZtdfMD0lTirA9gsQs
gGE
b)https://open.spotify.com/playlist/3FI9eznPQlBU6hLJQADNLg?fbclid=
IwAR3JoSBo6lLRw1x3ridXfizf8qeD6DSbFAfO_jiN9zUmCqpOWaLqg-
bl7To
c)https://open.spotify.com/playlist/1XQlFoQ9SHgOQFxmmehWYV?fbcli
d=IwAR0PTHoF1cfPtZIEbmipzwL4futxhrbqVDuXw1qy_gFBMKzItD3gz-
MARfg
(Note: Two songs in the playlist #3 above—"Universe" and "Get Lifted"—are synthesizer music which, though tolerable, is not usually recommended for deep experiential work.)

3) Suggestions from Jonathan Waller:
a) Jon Hopkins' (the artist, not the hospital) album, "Music for Psychedelic Therapy":
https://open.spotify.com/album/2zY5p176SfmupXceLKT6bH?si=ZWwM
TDraTjWwU9_Tjyv3Qw
b) Playlist compiled by Mendel Kaelen, who is widely regarded as an expert in this area, for Imperial College London's psilocybin therapy trials:
https://open.spotify.com/playlist/5u9GsOW8NpLJEqW8RzjdDz?si=50bd6
8f165164210
c) Album by East Forest called "Music for Mushrooms" which Jon personally found "a little bit too homogenous for an entire session but is very spacious, reas-suring and lovely, and has the added benefit of being five hours long, and very con-sistent throughout."
https://open.spotify.com/album/2LFyfGcBrrsvF8tECUs5gK?si=gFjVGUG
ASgy1rrmwxGqLIQ
d) Finally, this is a playlist Jon has collected of interesting instrumental albums, some of which may be good for sessions. Though a mixed bag, and with lots of synthesizer music in places, there may be many gems here—currently 57 hours of music.

https://open.spotify.com/playlist/4psMcIL3IBWXue2CHNv0tJ?si=aadff87
3091e457f

4) "Psilodep Session 2" by Rosalind Watts
https://open.spotify.com/playlist/1LBcs5ACHGjtmRs4vAnmLh

5) "Shamanic, tribal, drums, 5 Rhythms, yoga flow, slow motion" (27 hours of music): https://open.spotify.com/playlist/3PvNCpBRrnF79dm4U5zWbu

6) Two plant-medicine ceremony sets created by Deb Avery, on YouTube:
https://youtu.be/TkO5f9nit6g https://youtu.be/xsfyb1pStdw

My Research Article on the Solar-Galactic Macro-Astrology
www.archai.org/article-posts/the-solar-galactic-cycle-and-major-
watersheds-in-the-evolution-of-life. (Note: This will not be part of the course.)

Grof Legacy Training
www.grof-legacy-training.com

Academic Track - Ideas for Additional Research

Create a large natural zodiac wheel (Ascendant 0° Aries), which plots the planetary positions of all your close friends and family.

Keep a dream journal or look back at older dream journals and begin to correlate your dreams with your personal transits and the world transits.

Look back at any notable psychedelic sessions you have had and examine the trans-its for that day.

Follow your transits and/or the world transits for a period of between 3-30 days and note the synchronicities you observe.

Write a 250-word essay or make a video about a famous person, looking at their major aspects and some of the major themes in their personal and professional lives.

Write an essay or make a video about a natal aspect, comparing and contrasting the life experiences of several people who have that aspect.

Look at a world transit and explore the *synchronic* correlations (various manifesta-tions that occurred simultaneously during that transit) and/or *diachronic* correla-tions (manifestations that occurred during previous or subsequent world transits involving the same planetary archetypes).

II

The Birth of a New World View
(From *Pathways to Wholeness*)

Breakthrough in Europe

In the mid-1960s, Stanislav Grof, a young Czechoslovakian psychiatrist working at the Psychiatric Research Institute in Prague, made some extraordinary discoveries concerning the fundamental structures of the human psyche. Conducting sessions with a wide range of individuals in a program of systematic LSD psychotherapy, Grof and his clients encountered experiences that gradually and then irrevocably challenged the orthodox Freudian model in which he and his colleagues were working.

The experiences that emerged during these sessions suggested a far deeper understanding of the human psyche and the cosmos itself than had been previously imagined in any existing psychological theory. After supervising over 3000 sessions and studying the records of another 2000 from colleagues around the world, Grof eventually introduced a far-reaching new model that accounted for the observations of his clients' sessions, integrated a number of other psychological theories, and reached into areas of human spirituality described by the great mystical traditions of the world.

Grof's research, although representing a dramatic breakthrough in Western psychiatry and psychology, is supported by many precedents in non-Western and preindustrial societies. Since the dawn of history, guided *non-ordinary states of consciousness* have played a central role in the spiritual and ritual life of humanity. Stretching back more than 30,000 years, the shamans of ancient cultures began their healing professions through a spontaneous or induced experience of death and rebirth. In a firsthand way, they explored territories of the psyche that transcend the boundaries of normal individual awareness. Similarly, in the rites of passage, initiates were guided into non-ordinary—or what Grof terms *holotropic* (from *holos*, which means "wholeness"; and *trepein*, meaning "moving toward")—states of consciousness and had a personal experience of higher realms that transcend the physical world.

In the ancient mystery religions of the Mediterranean, neophytes participated in various mind-expanding processes in order to move beyond the limits of individual awareness and experience directly the sacred or *numinous* dimensions of existence. The celebrated Mother Goddess mysteries of Eleusis, for example, which were held near Athens for almost two-thousand years, we are now virtually certain used *ergot*, a naturally occurring form of LSD. Many of the creative and intellectual giants of Western culture, including figures such as Pythagoras, Plato, Aristotle, Epictetus, Euripedes, Sophocles, Plutarch, Pindar, Marcus Aurelius, and Cicero, all attest to the life-changing power of their experiences at Eleusis or one of the other mystery sites.

As well as the ritual use of psychedelic substances, many cultures around the world have used methods such as rhythmic drumming, trance dancing, sensory overload and sensory deprivation, sleep deprivation, breathing maneuvers, meditation, fasting, and other techniques to enter holotropic states. Preindustrial societies understood an important aspect of human nature that we in the modern West have forgotten: that exploring the psyche has the potential to mediate reconnection with the cosmic creative principle, helping people to overcome emotional and physical problems, transcend their fear of death, and reach a more integrated state of functioning in everyday life. Modern consciousness research, such as that conducted by Grof, has found that individuals who undergo these transformative processes automatically develop an interest in spirituality of a universal, non-sectarian, and all-encompassing nature. They also discover within themselves a sense of planetary citizenship, a high value placed on warm human relationships, and the urge to live a more simple and satisfying life in harmony with nature and ecological limits.

The considerable time and resources that other cultures devoted to finding effective techniques for exploring the inner terrains of the psyche is in marked contrast to the values in our modern industrial society. The dominant world view in Western civilization is concerned primarily with the external and physical layers of reality. In many ways it denies the existence of the human psyche altogether, and especially of higher spiritual or transpersonal states.

Grof's research thus provides an unexpected gateway to a deeper knowledge of the long neglected inner world. As we will see, the systematic exploration of the unconscious in holotropic states can initiate a profound transformation of awareness—a transformation that many now believe is urgently needed if we are to face and successfully overcome the great problems of our time. However, the journey into the heart of the psyche can be an immensely challenging process, exposing individuals to the depths and heights of human emotional experience. A map of the inner terrain, a way of understanding and predicting what might take place during holotropic-exploration sessions, would therefore be of invaluable benefit.

An Unexpected Rosetta Stone

For years, Grof and his colleagues had looked unsuccessfully for some kind of diagnostic system—such as the *Minnesota Multiphasic Personality Inventory* test (MMPI), Shostrom's *Personal Orientation Inventory* (POI), the *Rorschach Inkblot Test*, and others—to predict the experiences of their clients in deep self-exploration. Decades later, when the cultural historian Richard Tarnas discovered and systematically applied what Grof would later call the "Rosetta Stone" of archetypal astrology to this problem, Grof had to ironically concede that the one successful predictive technique turned out to be a system that was even more controversial and beyond the range of conventional science than his research in psychedelic therapy. Despite their deep initial skepticism toward astrology, however, the correlations that he and Tarnas observed were striking and consistent over time. Whether the catalyst was Grof® Breathwork, a psychoactive substance, or a spontaneous eruption of unconscious contents during a psychospiritual crisis, archetypal astrology provides, in Grof's words, "the only system that can successfully predict both the content and timing of experiences encountered in non-ordinary states of consciousness in experiential psychotherapy."

Given the widespread misunderstanding of and skepticism toward astrology in the modern era, a brief preface is required before we proceed. Although many of the founders of modern science, notably Johannes Kepler and Galileo Galilei, retained a deep belief in the principles as well as the practice of astrology, and of a higher cosmic intelligence or God, subsequent generations would later discard this understanding as the relic of an older mindset. Although the astrological vision became deeply discredited in the modern scientific West, the world view underlying it maintained credibility and continued to flourish in the philosophical movements of late Neoplatonism, Idealism, and Romanticism, in a direct lineage from Socrates and Plato.

This situation began to change in the mid-twentieth century, however, with the work of the pioneering psychiatrist C. G. Jung. Jung's discovery of the archetypes of the collective unconscious, his formulation of synchronicity ("an acausal connecting principle"), and his speculations concerning the *anima mundi* (world soul) provided a conceptual framework for the mature rebirth of a more psychologically oriented and nuanced form of astrology. Brought to fruition through the writing of figures such as Dane Rudhyar, Robert Hand, and Liz Greene, this new approach drew on the insights of Jungian depth psychology while leaving behind many of the old fatalistic dogmas of traditional astrological practice. Hand's work also set the stage for a much more rigorously self-critical and self-questioning discipline.

Then Grof's friendship and collaboration with Tarnas was to initiate another major leap in the field. A highly respected philosopher and psychologist, as well as historian, Tarnas gained international acclaim with his best-selling *The Passion of the Western Mind* (1991), which went on to become required reading in a number of university courses around the world. He followed this in 2006 with *Cosmos and Psyche,* in which he presented over five-hundred pages of systematic and compelling evidence to support his groundbreaking theory.

Tarnas begins by introducing the concept of archetypes that has played such an important role in the Western philosophical tradition. For now, we can describe the archetypes simply as primordial patterns of experience, which influence all people and cultures in the form of basic habit patterns, instincts and emotions. In *Cosmos and Psyche's* bold hypothesis, Tarnas suggests that the dynamic interplay of these timeless universals that have shaped our history occurs in coincidence with geometric alignments between the planets and the Earth, intelligible through an emerging epistemology and method of analysis which he calls *archetypal astrology.*

In contrast with traditional astrological belief and practice, the archetypal approach that Tarnas introduces is non-fatalistic and non-deterministic. The archetypes are recognized at all times as being complexly multivalent and multidimensional—taking different forms in different situations and at different times in people's lives. Each archetypal complex can manifest in a wide range of possible expressions, while still being true to its basic thematic character. Tarnas carefully demonstrates that the methodology he presents is *archetypally* predictive rather than *concretely* predictive. Although planetary alignments can illuminate many essential characteristics of an historical epoch or individual life experience, and even suggest basic expected characteristics of an upcoming period, he emphasizes that the specific concrete expression the archetypes will take at any time remains indeterminate—contingent on additional factors such as cultural context, free will, co-creative participation, and perhaps unmeasurables such as karma, grace, and chance.

It should be acknowledged that many of the fundamental tenets of the emerging archetypal world view concerning the nature of the human psyche and of the universe itself are compatible with the most recent branches of modern science, including quantum-relativistic physics, the holographic model of the brain, the study of morphogenetic fields and morphic resonance in biology, the study of dissipative structures, systems theory, chaos theory, cybernetics and information theory, the anthropic principle in astrophysics, and others. Grof also mentions the pioneering attempts of Ken Wilber and the successful accomplishment of Ervin Laszlo in integrating transpersonal psychology into a new comprehensive paradigm. I would further note Keiron Le Grice's work in *The Archetypal Cosmos*, which draws on the implications of Tarnas' research and integrates many of the new scientific theories in direct support of an archetypal or holotropic world view. Perhaps the most concise way to describe this emerging paradigm in science is the realization that consciousness, rather than being an accidental by-product of neurophysiological and biochemical processes in the brain, is an integral component of the universe itself.

The most well-known area of Tarnas' study to most readers has been his exploration of cyclically unfolding archetypal dynamics in human history and culture, deeply informed by the principles of Jungian and transpersonal depth psychology. A less widely known aspect of his inquiry, and the area on which this book concentrates, is based on his research with Grof into holotropic states of consciousness. In 1990, I proposed the term *holotropic astrology* to describe this facet of Tarnas' research that is specifically concerned with holotropic states.

Tarnas refers to astrology as a kind of "archetypal telescope" directed on the psyche, a way of understanding and contextualizing the material that emerges in deep self-exploration. Grof similarly concludes that the role of holotropic and psychedelic states of consciousness in psychology is comparable to that of the microscope in biology and the telescope in astronomy. When responsibly combined, the therapeutic effectiveness of these powerful magnifying processes of the psyche cannot be overstated. During my own four decades of research with workshops, consultations and personal experience, I have come to believe that archetypal astrology and holotropic exploration have the potential to revolutionize humanity's relationship with its deeper nature and help us to rediscover a more harmonious relationship with each other, the natural world, and the larger cosmos.

Tarnas' correspondence between the perinatal matrices and the archetypal meanings associated with the four outer planets thus had the effect of deepening the theory and practice of astrology. He succeeded in bridging the credible core of the old astrological traditions with the most recent advances in consciousness research, depth psychology, and psychiatry. Grof's expanded cartography of psyche not only integrates the entire range of biographical, perinatal, and transpersonal domains that routinely emerge in deep self-exploration but also shows how they are connected. Most importantly, his clinical research confirms that there is a *finite* amount of negative material in the individual psyche.

Techniques of therapy and self-exploration, as well as astrological counselling styles, which focus solely on the post-natal, *biographical* layer of the psyche—i.e., events from infancy to the present—are overlooking important sources of human problems in the perinatal and transpersonal domains of the psyche. They are also missing the powerful healing mechanisms that exist on those levels.

On the other hand, counselors who are familiar with the entire range of material that might emerge in their clients' inner lives are able to offer deeper levels of support. By recognizing the timing of specific thematic passages in the emotional death-rebirth cycle, they can remind their clients that, however challenging their experiences, "this too shall pass." Whatever someone is going through in the transformational journey, the key is to trust the process. Surrendering deeply to the feelings of depression and entrapment associated with Saturn and the early stage of labor (Grof's Basic Perinatal Matrix II), for example, automatically consumes their effect in the psyche and allows the material to move in a more liberating direction. Actively facing and giving expression to the volcanic energies of Pluto left over from the dynamic stage of labor (Grof's Basic Perinatal Matrix III) clears the pathway to rebirth and transcendence.

At the same time, therapists and sitters conducting powerful experiential sessions such as breathwork or psychedelic therapy will find that they can benefit from the insights of archetypal astrology. Planetary transits provide a wealth of information about the essential timing, intensity, and direction of psychological dynamics and, since the time of Jung himself, this knowledge has been used by professionals around the world to better understand their clients' emotional unfolding. I hope this book helps to advance the accessibility of holotropic exploration and archetypal astrology for both practicing therapists and the educated, dedicated public.

III

Basics of Archetypal Astrology

(From *The Astrology of Love and Relationships* and *The Archetypal Universe*)

Planetary Archetype	Abbreviation	Symbol
Sun	SU	☉
Moon	MO	☽
Mercury	ME	☿
Venus	VE	♀
Mars	MA	♂
Jupiter	JU	♃
Saturn	SA	♄
Uranus	UR	♅
Neptune	NE	♆
Pluto	PL	♇
Ascendant	AC	Asc

Aspects and Transits

Archetypal pairs are formed in a number of ways in human experience, including *aspects, midpoints, personal transits, world transits, relationship synastry,* and *relationship composite* alignments. These blendings of the planetary archetypes tend to be at the heart of serious, in-depth approaches to astrology and contain the most important and helpful information about people's emotional and relationship issues. The zodiac signs—Aries, Taurus, and so forth—resemble adjectives or adverbs which act on the essential archetypal energies represented by the Sun, Moon, and planets in aspect to each other. In archetypal astrology, we begin with alignments between the planets. We might then add sign and house insights, as they either modify, confirm, or add texture to the core planetary-aspect meanings.

It is clear, however, that the archetypal goddesses and gods permeate their meanings through every layer of astrology. Like a deepening fractal pattern, an inquiry into any part of this rich system of symbolic correspondences reveals the workings of a divine principle of fantastic creative brilliance, artistry, curiosity, love, and care.

Aspects

Aspects are the angular distance between planets, relative to the earth. Two planets are in aspect if they are in a significant relationship to each other in the sky when you were born—0° apart, 60° apart, 90°, and so on—which suggests that the archetypal qualities related to those planets will be combined and merged over the course of your lifetime.

For example, Venus and Jupiter 120 degrees apart are said to be in *trine*. People born with Venus trine Jupiter will tend to experience their Venusian impulses toward love, friendship, and beauty manifesting in harmonious ways with Jupiter's impulses toward growth, expansion, and higher values. Venus and Jupiter 60 degrees apart are in *sextile* with each other. The major aspects in astrology are the conjunction (0° apart), sextile (60°), square (90°), trine (120°), and opposition (180°). The sextiles and trines are sometimes referred to as *flowing* aspects, while the conjunctions, squares, and oppositions as *dynamic* aspects. There are a number of other minor aspects, the most often used being the semisextile (30°), semisquare (45°), sesquiquadrate (135°), and quincunx (150°).

Aspect	Degrees Apart	Abbreviation
conjunction	0	con
semisextile	30	ssx
semisquare	45	ssq
sextile	60	sex
square	90	squ
trine	120	tri
sesquiquadrate	135	sqq
quincunx	150	qui
opposition	180	opp

We also study alignments in which one planet is exactly midway between two other planets, referred to as *midpoints*. These are formed when one planet is equidistant from two other planets ($a=b/c$), blending together the meanings of all three of the corresponding archetypes. For example, Venus at the midpoint of Saturn and Pluto is written as: VE=SA/PL.

When two planetary archetypes are activated, they tend to engage and inflect each others' meanings from both directions. In Jupiter-Pluto pairings, for example, the Jupiter archetype can act on Pluto (Jupiter→Pluto)—amplifying, expanding and supporting positive resolutions (Jupiter) of the cycles of psychospiritual death-rebirth, transformation, and regeneration associated with Pluto. The Pluto archetype can also influence Jupiter (Pluto→Jupiter)—intensifying, deepening and compelling into manifestation the impulses toward growth and integration associated with Jupiter.

Personal Transits and World Transits

In much the same way, a *transit* occurs when a planet in the sky at the present time aligns with a natal planet—lighting up or activating the emotions, energies, and themes related to both the transiting and natal planets involved. Finally, *world transits* form when two or more planets in the sky at the present time align with each other. Their corresponding archetypal themes will then affect the entire collective psyche of humanity.

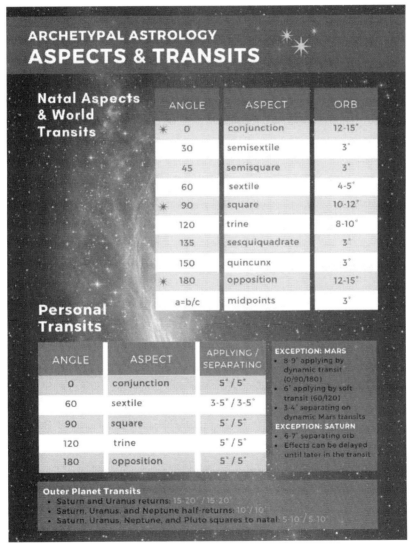

Fig. 1 Graphic by Lisa Leombruni.

Composite and Synastry Charts

A *composite* chart is a chart for the relationship itself, created by looking at the midpoints of both people's Suns, their Moons, and so forth. A *synastry* comparison is a side-by-side analysis of two charts. We look at how the planets in one person's chart interact with the planets in another person's chart.

Composite and synastry are the major techniques which astrologers use for looking at relationship dynamics. In general, we can say that synastry aspects indicate a range of emotional effects which you and your partner are likely to have on each other; whereas the composite chart depicts the relationship itself, resembling a third entity. Some astrologers see synastry aspects as more malleable and easier to resolve than those in composite charts. However, in archetypal astrology, we tend to see them as being similar in nature, with both synastry and composite aspects requiring ongoing self-exploration to resolve and integrate any problems associated with them.

I am indebted in this work to a discovery, in my formative years, of Robert Hand's volume on composite charts, *Planets in Composite.* Resembling his classic, *Planets in Transit,* I have found it to be a wise and helpful source of relationship understanding. I was also fortunate, early on, to read Frances Sakoian and Louis Acker's text on synastry, *The Astrology of Human Relationships.* Their writing, although richly laden with many profound and brilliant insights, has one foot solidly in the old fatalistic approach to astrology. For example, their descriptions of squares are almost unequivocally negative. The release of Sakoian and Acker's book, in the early 1970s, predated the spread of transpersonal psychology and the powerful holotropic approaches to resolving emotional problems which can help to turn our most challenging relationship aspects into catalysts for the greatest growth and healing.

In archetypal astrology, planetary pairs and triads are recognized as the primary carriers of meaning in the chart and some of the most important for new students to learn. People interested in a more complete introduction to the various technical issues in astrology will also benefit from reading Robert Hand's comprehensive *Horoscope Symbols* (1981).

Importance of the Perinatal Layer of the Psyche

The work of Grof and Tarnas has deepened the traditional understanding of astrology, by expanding and enriching those insights with observations from deep experiential psychotherapy and self-exploration. Essentially, any transit involving one of the planets Neptune, Saturn, Pluto, or Uranus will gain some of its core meaning from the perinatal matrix associated with that planet. These transits will also provide ongoing opportunities to work through leftover material from that stage of the death-rebirth process:

Neptune - *The Amniotic Universe*
Saturn - *Cosmic Engulfment and No Exit*
Pluto - *The Death-Rebirth Struggle*
Uranus - *Rebirth and Individuation*

The perinatal layer of the psyche—which contains unhealed birth trauma and fear of death—will for most people be one of the most dominant and pressing undercurrents in their life experience until it has been resolved and integrated. This material forms many of our most basic feelings about ourselves, other people, and the safety of the universe.

Archetypes

The concept of archetypes plays a fundamental role in astrology, as we have seen. Archetypes are universal patterns of experience, thought, or emotion. They are transcendent patterns which create and inform both the physical universe and our subjective experiences within it. The planets act as mirrors or reflections in the physical world of these higher cosmic principles. There are thus several layers of reality operative in astrology: the celestial bodies in the solar system, the archetypal forces to which they correspond, and our related human experiences.

In *Prometheus the Awakener*, Tarnas writes that archetypal principles can manifest in three broad realms of human experience and perception. They may take the form of:

Mythological principles – as described in world mythology, for example, the qualities of awareness and emotion personified by Shiva, Kali, Apollo, Aphrodite, Demeter, or Dionysus.

Philosophical principles – as explored in the writings of Plato, such as the Good, the Beautiful, and the True. These would also include fundamental universal polarities such as light and dark, or good and evil, and Pythagorean number symbolism such as the esoteric meanings associated with the numbers one, two, three, four, five, six, and so forth.

Psychological principles – as discovered by C. G. Jung, such as the anima and animus, the mother, the child, the wise old man, the lovers, the shadow, and the Self. We could also mention the archetypal terrains of paradise, heaven, hell, and purgatory and the psychological process of death and rebirth.

The central insight of astrology is that the activation of archetypal themes in our awareness occurs in regular coincidence with alignments between the planets. During a given planetary transit, we may perceive archetypal themes emerging through one, two, or all three of the dimensions of experience described above. We might feel emotions arising in our psyches (psychologically), observe our minds turning toward certain areas of thought (philosophically), or sense higher cosmic forces operating in our lives which seem to embody a numinous intelligence (mythologically and spiritually).

Multivalence and Variability of Expression

Another important principle in the emerging astrology is the variable or *multivalent* nature of planetary archetypes. Every aspect or transit has a wide range of possible expressions, while remaining true to its essential thematic nature. The exact concrete form an archetype will take is dependent on many additional factors, such as people's free will and creative intentions, their age and stage of life, the cultural context in which they live, the quality of relationship they have with their psyche, and as Tarnas suggests, perhaps unmeasurables such as karma and grace.

Thus, astrologers must take great care when looking at someone's birth chart, because we never know for sure what is going to happen or even what should happen. The most we can do is to offer a broad assessment of the range of possibilities which could emerge during a given period and some helpful ways to work with those energies and emotions. In general, the more people resolve their unconscious traumas, the easier it will be for them to navigate the twists and turns of daily existence and make wise, authentic, and life-supporting decisions.

IV

A Review of the Planetary Archetypes

Here below for the first time are my extended summaries of the individual planetary archetypes. I was originally going to include them in *The Archetypal Universe*, but decided to streamline that section of the book. Following the summaries, I review my longer writeups of the planetary archetypes from *The Archetypal Universe*. These are unique in that they explore both the meanings of the planetary archetypes in human life, as well as their relationship to the universal field of consciousness. Let's begin with the summaries.

Sun

Principles The conscious ego, impulses toward autonomy and selfhood, light and warmth, spirit and vitality, creative willpower and self-expression. - Tendencies toward self-centeredness and self-importance, an overbearing or domineering persona, yang energies dominating yin.

Character and Themes

Basic selfhood, personal identity, the conscious self. Energy, light, warmth, vitality, brightness, enthusiasm, celebration, play, "creative self-expression," the breath of life. Spirit, aspiration, purpose, willpower, confidence, leadership, the protagonist, the hero.

Shadow Qualities

Self-centeredness, self-importance, egotism, arrogance, big blind spots. Imbalance, an overly-yang, overbearing or domineering personality. An excess of purpose or willpower, burning oneself out.

Nature - Archetypes and Spirituality

Day, yang, life-force, summer, sunshine. - "Light of Divine essence," "Beauteous, bright creation," the Godhead, the Cosmic Sun, Brother Sun. Sun gods: Marduk (Babylon), Vishnu (India), Ra (Egypt); Helios, Apollo (Greece); Ahura Mazda (Persia), Sol (Gnosticism), Gawain (Celtic Europe). Hsi Ho (China), Shekina (Kabbalah). Plato's Idea of the Good. Atman, the individual self, the universal Self stepped down into the individual ego. The provider.
"I am . . ."
The Sun warms, vitalizes, and celebrates any archetype it combines with.

"Ye are the light of the world."

Moon

Principles Impulses toward nurture and mothering, rootedness and connection in a home, family and community, our capacity to feel, process, and reflect on our emotions, qualities of depth and soul. - Excessive emotionality and reactivity, moodiness or dependency, an unwillingness to grow up or leave home, indiscriminate helping instincts.

Character and Themes

Nurture, mother, childhood, home, family, roots, neighbors, the neighborhood, the community, the tribe, bloodlines, "we," "us," belonging, cocooning, connection, sharing. Sense of place. Earthly life, the rhythm of daily life and family life, biological rhythms, habit, instinct. Soul, emotion, compassion, sympathy, empathy, responsiveness. Homeland, motherland.

Shadow Qualities

Restlessness, impulsiveness, moodiness, activation of past emotional patterns, constant emoting. "Like wax receive, like marble retain": footprints on the Moon last for millions of years. Vulnerability, helplessness, dependency, never separating from the mother or leaving home.

Nature - The Arts

Night, yin, Sister Moon, the Earth, Mother Earth. The body, the "creature" part of us, clay, *prima materia*, containers. The fetus in utero, natural childbirth, midwifery, breast-feeding. Water, moistness. - Characterization, the medium of an art form, cohesion.

Archetypes and Spirituality

The Great Mother: Parvati (India), Inanna (Sumer), Ishtar (Babylon), Isis (Egypt), Rhea (Crete), Asherah (Middle East), Eve (Israel), Kuan-Yin (China), Kwannon (Japan); Demeter, Hecate, Hera, Alcmene (Greece); Cybele (Rome), Mary (Christianity), Freyja (northern Europe).

Mother of the Universe, Mother of Creation. The World Egg, cow-goddesses, moon goddesses: Chang-O, Hsi Wang Mu, Shin-Mu (China); Themis, Semele, Artemis, Phoebe, Europa (Greece); Minerva (Rome), Luna (Gnosticism), Fatima (Arabia), Hina (Polynesia). Moon gods: Apis (Egypt). Household deities, agriculture heroes, fertility deities, the earth's life-blood, sacred menstruation, Jahi (Persia). Anima, Psyche–"soul". The nurturer. The Church as mother.

"I feel . . ."

The Moon intimately feels and holds close any archetype it combines with.

"Earth, the mother of all life."

Mercury

<u>Principles</u> Impulses toward thought and communication, perception and observation, teaching and learning, movement and transportation, mental habits. - Tendencies toward an overly rational or one-sided point of view, the mind separated from human emotions, nervous overstimulation, excessive talking.

Character and Themes

Thought processes, ideas, understanding, communication, speech, writing, curiosity, study, reason, perception, point of view, modulation, deciphering, images. Decisions, details, distinctions, nuances, cleverness, dexterity. Errands, traveling short distances. Mental habits.

Shadow Qualities

Dry intellect, shallow communication, superficiality, trivia, gossip. An ability to communicate on an emotional level. Restlessness, nervousness, lack of concentration. Intellectual pride. Mental rigidity, literalism, pedantic thinking.

Nature - The Arts - Archetypes

Movement, communication. - Style, narrative. - Messengers of the gods: Thoth, Hermes. Odysseus, Mercurius. With Uranus: Trickster, Coyote, Monkey. With Pluto, the psychopomp: Anubis (Egypt), Hermes (Greece), Woden-Odin (northern Europe). Animus. Objective observation of one's mind.

"I think . . ."

Mercury creates a mental interest in and communication channel for any archetype it combines with.

"Hermes, the winged messenger of the gods."

Venus

Principles Impulses toward love and friendship, harmony and pleasure, grace and beauty, forces of attraction. - Social pretensions and shallowness, vanity and conceit, self-indulgence and laziness, cravings for sugar as a substitute for love.

Character and Themes

Love, beauty, grace, harmony, tenderness, attraction, sensuality, pleasure, the passive and receiving aspects of sexuality. Loved ones, friends, fun, connecting, socializing. Higher unions of love, friendship and cooperation. Diplomacy, manners. Yin.

Shadow Qualities

Vanity, conceit, prestige, shallowness, phoniness, social materialism, cloying sweetness or friendliness, beauty overdone, the beautiful people. Laziness, passivity, indulgence, extravagance, excess intake of sugar and sweets. False happiness, romantic illusions.

Nature - The Arts

Love, beauty, attraction. - Color, harmony, taste, aesthetic sense. The elegance or aesthetic appeal of a theory. Artists, troubadours, art for art's sake, epicureanism.

Archetypes and Spirituality

The goddess of love: Lakshmi (India), Nu Kua (China), Inanna (Sumer), Ishtar (Babylon), Hathor (Egypt); Aphrodite, Helen, Psyche (Greece); Venus (Rome). Beauty: Europa, Adonis (Greece). The feng-huang: the Chinese phoenix, totem of music and weddings.

With the Moon: *philia*. With Mars: Eros-Cupid. With Neptune: *agape*. The yoni: the sexual power of the feminine. - Plato's Idea of the Beautiful. Divine Love, the Beloved, love as the desire to regain spiritual wholeness.

"I enjoy . . ."

Venus brings grace and harmony to any archetype it combines with.

It is impossible to live pleasurably without living wisely, well, and justly, and impossible to live wisely, well, and justly without living pleasurably.

Diogenes

Pleasure is the beginning and the end of living happily.

Epicurus

Love is perfect kindness.
    Joseph Campbell

Mars

Principles Impulses toward action and assertion, energy and passion, the dynamic pursuit of goals and objectives, urges to protect oneself in times of danger. - Tendencies toward selfish gratification, competitive drive and excessive use of force, feelings of anger and aggression.

Character and Themes

Energy, action, self-assertion, strength, courage, directness. "The urge to define oneself through interaction." Sports, athletic energy, passion, the dynamic aspects of sexuality. Yang.

Shadow Qualities

Competition, the urge to be first, physical overexertion, headstrong or pointed energy, audacity, impulsiveness, conflict, anger, aggression, rash actions, warlike energy, fight or flight. Selfish gratification. Itching, burning.

Nature - The Arts

Active self-preservation, hunting, posturing. The sexual impulse, heat. - Artistic passion, fervor. Themes of conflict.

Archetypes and Spirituality

Gods and goddesses of war: Ishtar, Athena, Ares, Mars, Minerva. Cain, Achilles. The lingam: the sexual power of the masculine. Aiming one's aggressive energies at transcendence: the space above and beyond conflict.
"I pursue . . ."
Mars energizes and asserts any planet it combines with.

"Glorious Hector held out his
arms to his baby,
who shrank back to his fair-girdled nurse's
    bosom
screaming, and frightened at the aspect of his own
    father,
terrified as he saw the bronze and the crest with
    its horsehair,

nodding dreadfully, as he thought, from the peak
 of the helmet."
 Iliad VI, trans. R. Lattimare
 (The son of Hector, the Trojan champion, is terrified by his father's armor.)

Jupiter

Principles   Impulses toward growth and expansion, optimism and generosity, tolerance and acceptance of others, broadened experience and integration into larger wholes. - Tendencies toward inflation and excess, pride and arrogance, self-righteousness and sense of entitlement.

Character and Themes

Expansion, growth, optimism, joviality, well-being, joy. Opportunities, broadened experience, integration into a larger whole, "incorporating more of the universe into one's experience," broad vision. Resources, generosity, sharing, reaching out, integrity, trust, freedom.

The great liberal tradition, liberal values, truth, belief, faith, syncretism. Traveling long distances, higher education, philosophy, exploration of other cultures, multiculturalism. A feeling of fortune, saving grace, prosperity, surplus. The opportunity to manifest and act out whatever archetypal energies Jupiter is influencing.

Shadow Qualities

Materialism, inflation, greed, excess, waste, envy, hypocrisy, privilege, being spoiled or born with a silver spoon in one's mouth. Pride, arrogance, self-righteousness, pretension, prestige, putting on airs, "Mr. Big." Glory, pomp, grandeur. "Knowledge puffeth up." With Uranus: delusions of genius. With Neptune: delusions of enlightenment. With Pluto: delusions of superiority.

Nature - The Arts - Archetypes

Growth, propagation, the cosmos. - Artistic scope, size, liberality. - The Great Benefic, Zeus in his role as the grand, generous, and just king of the gods on Mt. Olympus. Athena, Apollo. Plato's Idea of the True. Providence, guardian angels. Blessings, prosperity and good-fortune deities: Lakshmi, Ganesh (India); the dragon, Lu Hsing, Ts'ai Shen (China); Hecate (Greece). The Wheel of Fortune, Lady Luck, Mammon. - The tendency to feel spiritually superior to others, the ego's need to be one of God's chosen few, the chosen people.

"I amplify . . ."

Jupiter expands, broadens, and potentially inflates any archetype it combines with.

Prosperity tries the souls of even the wise.
   Sallust

To go beyond is as wrong as to fall short.
    Confucius

There is no calamity greater than lavish desires.
There is no greater guilt than discontentment.
And there is no greater disaster than greed.
    Lao Tzu

It is easier for a camel to go through the eye of a needle, than for a rich man to enter into the kingdom of God.
    Jesus

A people . . . which say, Stand by thyself, come not near to me; for I am holier than
thou.
    Isaiah

Jupiter says, "I will give you an abundance of opportunities. Half of them will be
really good ideas and half will be illusory seductions, tailor-made to fool you."
    Caroline W. Casey, *Making the Gods Work for You*

Saturn

Principles Incarnation in material form, real-world concerns and responsibilities, work and structure, time and boundaries, qualities of maturity and wisdom, patience and forbearance. - Forces of constriction and hardening, boundaries and separation, problems and challenges, repression and defensiveness, fearful enslavement to the past.

Character and Themes

Form, structure, boundaries, differentiation, the mature ego, the embodied self. Tests of patience and forbearance, responsibility, integrity, focus, priorities, realism, a straightforward approach to life, "exchanging a great dim possibility for a small concrete reality." Work, discipline, duty, performing one's *dharma*, humility. Tradition, conservatism, caution, prudence, temperance, fortitude, thoughtful people with balanced egos, the conscience, dignity, austerity, reserve. "Coming of age." Karmic law, mortality, the inevitability of death, the preciousness of time. Matter, density, gravity.

Shadow Qualities

Constriction, contraction, limitation, inhibition, alienation, parts isolated from the whole. Frustration, defeat, pessimism, sacrifice, victimization, fear, pain, traumas, engrams, armor, skandhas (layers of unconsciousness), hangups. The bony side of life, rigidity, crystallization, intolerance, sad loners, "the process of hardening up," sphincter control, the inner parent, the inner tyrant, superego, introjected birth canal. The body as the primary measure of individual being. "The whips and scorns of time," fate and heredity, endings, the convincing illusion of death as an ending.

Philosophical minimalism, quantification, unbalanced objectivity, materialistic monism, the mechanistic vision of the universe, the universe as a supermachine. Logical positivism, existentialism, secularism, atheism.

Nature - The Arts

The survival instinct, self-preservation. Winter, consolidation, the dying of the old. Long-term processes and development. - Form, rhythm, convention, inertia. Realism, naturalism. Sombre or depressing themes.

Archetypes and Spirituality

The contraction of spirit into matter, involution, dualism, dichotomy and separation between self/other, inner/outer, subject/object, human/world. God as absolute unreachable other, absolutisms, monotheism, "death of God" theology. Spiritual literalism, the physical Resurrection. Lower *maya, samsara, jivas,* the *demiurge* (creator of the material universe), Li, Tezcatlipoca, the illusion of small 'r' consensus reality, Plato's Cave, "rush hour, hamburger-stand consciousness."

Sin, the Fall, the curse, banishment, loss of paradise, the crucifixion in matter, the World Tree, the shadow of death. Jahweh the stern lawgiver, the harsh taskmaster, the covenant with an exacting God, eye-for-an-eye justice, fear of God, the Prophet as warner, "fear is the mother of morals," "Thou shalt." The Road of Trials, the Way of the Cross, shame and guilt cultures. Miserable sinners, the downtrodden, judgment by the jealous God. Shang Ti, Ouranos, Kronos, Zeus as tyrant. The *senex.* Moira, Ananke (Necessity), Dike (Justice), Heimarmene (Alotted Fate), Nemesis (Retribution), Atropos (the Cutter), Mara, the Sphinx: "sphincter, strangler," Tartaros. The fallen age, the Age of Iron, the Spirit of Gravity, Father Time, the Grim Reaper, Thanatos, fear of being swallowed by the *vagina dentata.* The Old Goat.

Grof's *Basic Perinatal Matrix II* (Tarnas). Cosmic engulfment, hell, "no-exit," unbearable suffering that will never end. Identification with victims of all times and places. Guilt, doubt, hopelessness, helplessness, feelings of entrapment and encagement, inhibited or endogenous depression. The hylotropic impulse: "moving toward matter." Paying off karma, learning important lessons, the karmic eye of the needle.

"I take seriously…"

Saturn structures and focuses serious attention on any archetype it combines with.

In order to create the phenomenal worlds, the Divine has to abandon its original state of pristine undifferentiated unity. Considering how fantastic the experience of identification with Absolute Consciousness is from the human perspective, it seems strange that the creative principle should seek an alternative, or at least a complement, to a simple experience of itself…. What could possibly motivate the Divine to seek separation, pain, struggle, incompleteness, and impermanence, in short, precisely the states from which we are trying to escape when we embark on the spiritual journey?. . .

[According to the insights of individuals in holotropic states of consciousness] Spirit has a profound desire to experience what is opposite and contrary to its own nature. It wants to explore all the qualities that in its pristine nature it does not have and to become everything that it is not. Being eternal, infinite, unlimited, and ethereal, it longs for the ephemeral, impermanent, limited by time and space, solid, and corporeal.

Stanislav Grof, *The Cosmic Game*

Here, on both the individual and the collective levels can be seen the source of the profound dualism of the modern mind: between man and nature, between mind and matter, between self and other, between experience and reality—that pervading sense of a separate ego irrevocably divided from the encompassing world. Here is the painful separation from the timeless all-encompassing womb of nature, the development of human self-consciousness, the loss of connection with the matrix of being, the expulsion from the Garden, the entrance into time and history and materiality, the disenchantment of the cosmos, the sense of total immersion in an antithetical world of impersonal forces.... For an unconscious person, the full reality of human bondage is fearfully repressed and is therefore all the more omnipotent in its impoverishment of life.

    Richard Tarnas, *The Passion of the Western Mind*, referring to the Saturnian features of the birth process (especially Grof's Basic Perinatal Matrix II).

To grunt and sweat under a weary life.
    Shakespeare

Life is one long struggle in the dark.
    Lucretius

Must not all things at the last be swallowed up in death?
    Plato

I have seen the moment of my greatness flicker,
And I have seen the eternal Footman hold my coat, and snicker,
And in short, I was afraid.
    T. S. Eliot

This rite of initiation, with its revelation of father first as ogre and persecutor, its requirement of acceptance of the 'rules' and conditions of the world, and its ultimate vision of a merciful Father and an immortal soul, seems to be the archetypal Saturnian path.... Each thing that is worth having must be approached by the route that winds past the throne of the Father.

    Liz Greene, *Saturn: A New Look at an Old Devil*

He who cannot obey himself will be commanded.
    Friedrich Nietzsche

Exploring the Archetype of Hell

    Tarnas talks about the three most extreme forms of archetypal hell: Saturn-Uranus, the hell of unbearable tension; Saturn-Neptune, the hell of nightmarish uncertainty; and Saturn-Pluto, the hell of breakdown and decay. Other variations of the hell archetype include Sun-Saturn, the hell of inhibited self-expression; Moon-Saturn, the hell of isolation and personal deficiency; Mercury-Saturn, the hell of repetitive negative thinking; Venus-Saturn, the hell of rejection and vanity; Mars-Saturn, the hell of frustration; and Jupiter-Saturn the hell of lost opportunity.

These are the shadow sides of the archetypes. When people allow themselves to surrender to and deeply feel the painful emotions related to Saturn, they automatically transmute its energies into more constructive forms. Saturn will then manifest as tempered and disciplined creativity (Sun-Saturn), routine and disciplined self-reflection (Moon-Saturn), careful and disciplined thought (Mercury-Saturn), deliberate and disciplined enjoyment (Venus-Saturn), tempered and disciplined action (Mars-Saturn), slow and disciplined expansion (Jupiter-Saturn), responsible and disciplined change (Saturn-Uranus), applied and disciplined spirituality (Saturn-Neptune), and systematic and disciplined transformation (Saturn-Pluto).

Uranus

Principles Impulses toward freedom and awakening, rebirth and breakthroughs, experimentation and rebellion, innovation and originality, individuation and independence. - Manic and erratic restlessness, excessive needs for in-dependence and autonomy, an inability to cooperate or compromise, unwillingness to work within structures or commit, states of extremism, fanaticism and hubris.

Character and Themes

Freedom, breakthroughs, rebirth, redemption, "the sudden unexpected reso-lution of difficult situations," the chance to redeem the past, sudden openings, new opportunities, "Eureka!" excitement, inspiration, what turns us on in life, optimism. Independence, individuation, self-actualization, eccentricity, inspired loners. Rebel-lion, experimentation.

Higher mind, intelligence, genius, electrifying inspiration, illumination, bril-liance, crystal clarity, lucid insight, "the smile of reason," the union of intelligence and spirituality, the spiritual or intellectual midwife. "Genius is the woman in man." Inhalation.

Chance, the unexpected, the unpredictable element in the universe, the uncer-tainty principle, the wild card. Eternal change, the fulfilled dialectic.

Shadow Qualities

Mania, incomplete rebirth, erratic behavior, quirkiness, impatience, chronic problems with authority figures, inability to cooperate, unwillingness to tolerate structure or limitation of any kind, unwillingness to commit, an excessive urge for freedom, freedom for its own sake, flash-in-the-pan rebellion, rebelling against the wrong things, fool's gold, false breakthroughs. - Hubris, inflation, "Christ complex," delusions of genius.

Nature - The Arts

Lightning, springtime, melting snow, the end of a storm or drought, birth. Reaching a new level of development. - Humanism, innovation, the avant-garde. Impressionism, abstract or conceptual art, futurism.

Archetypes and Spirituality

The liberator and discoverer: Prometheus, Fu Hsi, Huang Ti, the Awakener, the Rebel, the Trickster, the Eternal Child, the *puer*, the Divine Child. Persephone as bringer of new life, Zeus as liberator. The magical birth of heroes, the Knight Errant, Robin Hood, slaying the dragon, capturing the Golden Fleece. Lady

Liberty, liberating fire, hatred of tyrants, "Let my people go," Ch'ih Yu's revolt against heaven. The archetype of the Messiah, savior-redeemer gods: Krishna, Osiris, Hou I, Attis, Mithra, Christ. Death of the inner tyrant, "the God who knows how to dance," "Welcome, O life!"

The birth of Christianity after the brutality of the Roman Empire, the birth of science (the Enlightenment) after the brutality of Christian sectarian warfare and the Inquisition, the birth of the emerging transpersonal paradigm after the environmental and spiritual brutality of mechanistic science. The conversion experience, rediscovery of the Divine, exaltation, enlightenment, satori. "To become as God," "I and the Father are one," atonement, immanent divinity. Miracles, eternity overcoming time, "I once was blind, but now I see," "Light of heaven." - Dreams of four objects or four people (including oneself) and dreams of houses, squares or circles (mandalas) signify the completion of a growth cycle and a new wholeness of the inner Self (Jung).

Grof's *Basic Perinatal Matrix IV* (Tarnas). Ego death and rebirth, separation from the mother. Delivery, deliverance, redemption, forgiveness. Reconnection with the Great Mother, God, or the Divine in a more abstract form such as radiant light or a loving presence. Illuminative or Promethean type of ecstasy. Dramatic healing, disappearance of symptoms, feelings of success, transcendence, awakening. Brotherly and sisterly feelings. Desire to live a simple and satisfying life with "minimum consumption, maximum satisfaction." Urge for meaningful work and synergy with others to solve problems. Sparkling world, universal redemption. Critical attitudes toward the abuse of power.

"I am liberated through . . ."

Uranus awakens, excites, and liberates any archetype it combines with and reveals the emancipatory qualities of that archetype.

After the subject has experienced the limits of total annihilation and "hit the cosmic bottom," he or she is struck by visions of blinding white or golden light. The claustrophobia and compressed world of the birth struggle suddenly opens up and expands into infinity. The general atmosphere is one of liberation, salvation . . . and love.

Stanislav Grof, on the experience of ego death and rebirth in deep, systematic self-exploration.

Verily, verily I say unto thee, except a man be born again, he cannot see the kingdom of God . . . Except ye . . . become as little children, ye shall not enter into the kingdom of heaven.

Jesus

Every valley shall be exalted, and every mountain and hill shall be made low: and the crooked shall be made straight, and the rough places plain.

Isaiah

Failure is impossible.
  Susan B. Anthony

What another would have done as well as you, do not do it. What another would have said as well as you, do not say it; written as well, do not write it. Be faithful to that which exists nowhere but in yourself—and thus make yourself indispensable.
  André Gide

Improvement makes straight roads; but the crooked roads without improvement are roads of genius.
  William Blake

Neptune

Principles Yearnings for higher meaning and connection, openings of vision and imagination, sympathy and compassion, feelings of serenity and bliss, cosmic unity. - Tendencies toward escapism or confusion, illusion and deception, false mirages of security and satisfaction, toxic-womb feelings.

Character and Themes

Spirituality, vision, imagination, inspiration, intuition, meaning, Logos. The inner life, dreams, fantasy, mystery, enchantment, appreciation. Feelings of unity, connection, mysticism, no boundaries, dissolving, surrender, letting go, merging, absorption, blending of realities, other dimensions.

Peace, serenity, tranquility, divine relaxation, higher nurture, melted ecstasy, reunion with the source, ablution, atonement. Compassion, service, faith. Exhalation.

Shadow Qualities

Confusion, deception, self-deception, escapism, illusion. Projection of the Divine in spiritual, romantic, or materialistic mirages. Narcissism, "uroboric incest," the desire to return to the archetypal ocean but in mistaken, unhealthy, and ineffective ways, addiction. Vulnerability, weakness, dissipation, dissolution, paranoia.

Nature - The Arts

Space, ocean, water, mist, fog, gentle breeze. - The Muses, Higher Beauty, ethereal, mystical or spiritual art. Iconism, symbolism, allegory, fantasy, surrealism, abstraction, flowing forms.

Archetypes and Spirituality

The numinous, the Divine, the Infinite, the Macrocosmic or Supracosmic Void that is empty yet all-containing, Cosmic Emptiness and Nothingness, the "Beyond Within." The yoni, the womb of existence, cradle of all dimensions in the universe, the Deep, Tiamat, Oceanus, the face of the waters, "In the beginning was the Word." The Universal Mind, the Great Mother, the mother of the universe, God, the godhead, Brahman, the Tao, Buddha nature, *dharmadhatu*: "ultimate reality." Sophia, Shekhina, Ch'ung, Quetzalcoatl, the Great Manitou, the Great Soul, the Oversoul, the universal essence, higher *Maya*, *Lila*: divine play. The indestructible jewel, nirvana, *sunyata*, the rock that the wise man or woman builds their house upon, the New Jerusalem (i.e., an inner sacred state of consciousness rather than an external place).

Unus mundus: one world, "all things are the same," "indivisible, yet . . . divided among beings," cosmic unity, the blanket of Indra. *Geist*, self-subsistent meaning, self-subsistent Being, the Unknowable, "the irrepresentable space-time continuum," the timeless aeons of prehistory, "the vast ground of silence," eternity. Cosmos. Pantheism, the Fool, the number zero, the mandala (circular patterns): symbol of spiritual wholeness. "The human love affair with the Divine," "the goal of human life is to see God." Divine Grace.

Grof's *Basic Perinatal Matrix I* (Tarnas). The amniotic universe, the biological, emotional, and spiritual union of fetus and mother in utero. The union of soul and Divine. Also "toxic womb" experiences. Oceanic or Apollonian type of ecstasy. Heaven, paradise, *unio mystica*, "Thou art that," *atman-Brahman* union.

"I am enchanted by . . ."

Neptune sensitizes and spiritualizes any archetype it combines with.

The experience of cosmic unity is characterized by transcendence of the usual subject-object dichotomy. The individual in this state becomes deeply aware of his or her unity with other people, nature, and the entire universe, and with the ultimate creative principle, or God. This is accompanied by an overwhelming positive affect that can range from peace, serenity and bliss to an ecstatic rapture.... This state of mind is referred to as "contentless yet all containing," "formless but pregnant with form," one of "cosmic grandeur yet utmost humility," or characterized by loss of ego while at the same time the ego has expanded and become the whole universe. Different subjects experience and describe this event within different symbolic frameworks. Most frequent references are to Paradise, The Garden of Eden, Heaven, Elysian Fields, unio mystica, the Tao, Atman-Brahman union, or Tat Tvam Asi (Thou art That).

Stanislav Grof, *LSD Psychotherapy*

The kingdom of God is within you.
    Jesus

God dwells within you as you.[1]
    Tenet of Siddha Yoga

Look within, you are the Buddha.
    Buddhist scriptures

You are of divine nature.
    Upanishads

---

[1] This and the next four quotes appeared in Grof's *The Cosmic Game*.

Heaven, earth and human are one body.
  Tenet of Confucianism

The first of gods, the ancient Soul . . . the supreme Resting-place of the universe
. . . the Knower and That which is to be known and the Ultimate Goal.
  Bhagavad Gita, describing Brahman, the Supreme Reality in Hinduism.

We are not human beings trying to have a spiritual experience. We are a part of one
spiritual Being having all the experiences.
  The perennial philosophy

Einstein is God impeccably impersonating Albert Einstein and a chimpanzee is
God playing perfectly the role of a chimpanzee.
  Stanislav Grof

The Numinous is a category which exists totally outside of conventional science's comprehension. Yet it is the one category of experience which is dearer to
the human soul than any other, for the Numinous is the repositor of all meaning,
the reason for our existence, the Logos…. This most unsubstantial and blithe of
realities is in truth the most absolute controller of consciousness, the true creative
dictator of the psyche's conditions. Even the most finite and unimaginative hard-
as-nails perception is a visionary play of the infinite Imagination.
  Richard Tarnas, *Prometheus the Awakener* (unpublished long version)

Pluto

Principles Processes of breakdown, destruction and creation in the universe, impulses toward regeneration and transformation, purification and purging, profound evolutionary forces. - Brutal and ruthless behaviors, driving obsessive energies, the underworld side of the psyche, volcanic feelings.

Character and Themes

Evolution, transformation, regeneration, the forces of nature and history, sex and procreation. Consciousness-force, primal energy, intensity. The dying and renewal of what is outmoded, destruction of old forms and rebirth of new ones. Purging, burning away the past, what is unconscious being pushed up into consciousness, the "cosmic rototiller."

Reinforcement, building up again after a crisis, titanic forces of renewal. The orgasm as "little death," sexuality as "an overwhelming natural force of cosmic dimensions." The intrusive cosmic force pressing the baby out of the birth canal.

Shadow Qualities

The Id, the dark side, the *kleshas:* instinctual forces. Aggression, brutality, ruthlessness, obsession, compulsion, forcing change or changes forced on one. Heavy energy, power and domination, fear. Hell breaking loose, catharsis. The relationship between indulgence in and transcendence of the material world. Vulgarity, the fetid side of life, seediness, the connection between decay and new life.

Nature - The Arts

The cosmic force driving the processes of sexuality, aggression, destruction, death, decay, regeneration, and renewal. Fall, Halloween. - Expressionism, Fauvism.

Archetypes and Spirituality

Divine Will, the active form of Absolute Consciousness, the force that compels all forms to rise out of and disappear back into Neptune's Metacosmic Void, creative cosmic consciousness, the Prime Mover, the demiurge: creator of the material universe. The *lingam*. Shiva, Kali, Shakti: cosmic or universal energy, kundalini, Kama-Mara: "Desire-Death," Dionysus, Pan, Hades, Demeter-Earth as swallower of her own daughter Persephone, the "phallic mother," Zeus as rapist. Wild nature: Artemis, Poseidon, Charon, the Minotaur, the Hydra, the harpies, maenads, satyrs, the Clash of the Titans. Sauron, Mordor.

Old Testament tribal genocides, the Slaughter of the Innocents, the Inquisition. The archetypes of the Apocalypse, Armageddon, the lake of fire and brimstone. Sodom and Gomorrah, orgies and sacrifice to the golden calf while Moses is on Mt. Sinai, fallen angels. The Eucharist: symbolic eating of Christ's body and drinking His blood (this ritual is a carry-over from eras when many human groups ritually killed and ate their king after a predetermined interval of rulership). Walking through the valley of the shadow of death. - Dreams of five people (including oneself) indicate there is an ego-humbling in progress, i.e., one's own limiting selfhood stands in the way of the experience of the number four, which symbolizes wholeness.

Grof's *Basic Perinatal Matrix III* (Tarnas). The death-rebirth struggle, purgatory, volcanic or Dionysian type of ecstasy. Confrontation with the inner themes of titanic aggression, sadomasochism, scatology, the demonic, and pyrocathartic (purification by fire). Identification with both victims and perpetrators. Active or exogenous depression, struggle to spiritually die and be reborn. Birth "down and through." Fate = unresolved experiences of the deep unconscious (the perinatal). Fate as just another archetype, which can be consumed in a flow of perinatal experience.

"I confront my shadow and am regenerated through..."

Pluto compels whatever archetype it combines with into manifestation with enormous force.

The moral constrictions of Saturn's judgmental and defensive view of Nature, sexuality, and the elemental instincts is transformed into the full Plutonic awareness of all instincts and all of Nature being a sacramental expression of the Divine Shiva.... The Grim Reaper, the weight of the world, the Old Testament god Yahweh, is suddenly recognized at a more profound level as Shiva, pressing his foot relentlessly on the baby to bring liberation.

Richard Tarnas, *Prometheus the Awakener*, unpublished long version

Pluto as an image of the dark maternal roots of the psyche is forever pulling us out of life and back into the womb of the Mother, either for renewal or death.

Liz Greene

Only the man who goes through this darkness can hope to make any further progress.

C. G. Jung

The Planetary Archetypes
(from *The Archetypal Universe*)

⊙   ## Sun

The archetypal complex related to the Sun informs our sense of individual autonomy and selfhood, and our impulses to shine, fully become, and express ourselves. It manifests through our psyches as light and warmth, vitality and enthusiasm, our yearnings for joy, celebration, and play, and our sense of creative purpose. The shadow qualities of the Sun archetype, including a self-centered or overbearing persona, can be overcome as we remember that all feelings of creative empowerment ultimately come through us from a higher source and are meant for the good of all.

Each planetary archetype also affects the ways in which we perceive that which is beyond ourselves, our sense of the divine principle, Goddess, or God. The Sun represents our experience of the divine as radiant, shining, and warming, as brilliant light, or as the breath of life itself. The solar aspects of divinity illuminate and inspire us, encourage, lead and light the way. The Sun also represents our sense of the Godhead as located in a particular transcendent locale, as shining forth from that central position, and as a good and positive force in the world. We can participate in the Sun's radiant outpouring through our own creative self-expression, including the act of having children.

From a transpersonal perspective, we could say that the Sun archetype represents that part of cosmic consciousness which has impulses to shine forth and create, to express its warmth, enthusiasm, and selfhood in the manifestation of new worlds, and to embody some of these same qualities in the beings it creates: imparting in them feelings of yang life-force, confidence, autonomy, and free will. The cosmic creative principle also seems to need, some of the time, to obscure this light in order to keep its presence fresh and appreciated—in the same way that sunny days are more enjoyable after those of darkness and rain.

☽   ## Moon

Just as the Sun archetype informs our identity as an autonomous, self-motivated, and creative being, the archetypal complex related to the Moon is behind our yearnings to be rooted in a home, a family, and community, to have a sense of "we" rather than only "I". The Moon symbolizes our needs to connect and hold close, to belong and include, nurture and be nurtured, and to support others by reflecting back the light of their own life force. It governs our legitimate human needs for warmth and contact, as well as our ability to care for the needs of others.

Similarly, whereas the Sun archetype is connected with our active, daytime, waking consciousness, the Moon rules relaxation, sleep, and night. It is our reflective and feeling function, our capacity to absorb and digest the experience of our daytime lives, to slow down, receive, and open to the emotional interiority of the world. Moistening and softening, the Moon symbolizes the replenishing rainfall of our feeling nature that leaves the soil of awareness ever fertile and life-supporting. As we access the heart of this archetype, we learn to supplement the Moon's tender caring for our own children and family, with the same emotions for all humanity and all living things.

The Moon represents our experience of Absolute Consciousness as kind and caring, as having compassion for our human pain and as loving us in a maternal way, looking out for us as something resembling its own children. The Moon suggests our capacity to feel a personal relationship with the sacred, to be held close in our imperfect creaturehood and merely human state, and not just as a spiritual being. It also represents the eternal feminine presence we can perceive deep within us, as *soul*.

From the transpersonal side, we might suggest that the Moon represents that part of divine consciousness which has impulses to give birth to separate beings which it can nurture and appreciate. The lunar archetype may also reflect the divine's enjoyment, shared with us, of our own close family relationships.

☿   Mercury

Mercury corresponds to the archetypal principles of thought and communication, our faculties of perception and insight, and our awareness of sensory stimuli. It manifests through our impulses to teach, transmit, and share information with the people around us. Enhancing a sense of distinctions, subtleties, and nuances, Mercury governs our curiosity about the world, our capacities to reason and conceptualize, to see the archetypal and mathematical order within things, and to enjoy games, puzzles, and wordplay. It is also connected with manual dexterity and transportation, especially everyday travel.

Spiritually, Mercury represents the power of the spoken or written word to evoke a perception of higher truths within us, and our capacity to share those insights with others. Overlapping with the Jupiter, Saturn, and Neptune archetypes, it manifests through the philosophical treatises and religious texts passed down to us from history, many with multiple levels of interpretation. Some of these meanings are meant for an everyday, *exoteric* perception of the world, and others for more mystical and *esoteric* levels of understanding. Mercury also rules the process of mindful meditation, as people observe the flow of thoughts passing through their awareness without either holding on to or fearing those thoughts, while also beginning to identify with the conscious divine space between them.

The Mercury as well as Saturn archetypes seem to underlie the tendency of many religious groups toward sectarian dogma, literalism, and fundamentalism. The solution to these problems is, Joseph Campbell writes, to remember that every religious deity, image, or passage in a book is just a doorway to a higher, formless level of divine consciousness. As people awaken, they learn to "see through" the surface layer of their own culture's version of the truth, to the common spiritual root which is in agreement with the mystical teachings of all times and places.

From the transpersonal side, we can say that Mercury represents that part of the Universal Mind which conveys feedback to humanity, which seems to instruct and communicate with us. Mercury also symbolizes the Godhead's imparting of mathematical and archetypal order throughout the universe, something like a cosmic blueprint or Logos (described as "In the beginning was the Word" in the Judeo-Christian tradition) and which enables human beings to comprehend those meanings. It also represents the capacity of Absolute Consciousness to be aware of every part of itself simultaneously: offering feedback, making adjustments, and responding to input and changes in the human-divine relationship. But like an interesting movie, the divine principle does not seem to want to give away its secrets too quickly, and we might suggest that the lower forms of the Mercury archetype underlie the tendencies in the human mind toward trivia, avoidance, and distraction.

Mercury also represents the Universal Mind's enjoyment of the incredibly diverse forms of communication among the world's living things, as the long ascent of humanity's writing and phonic skills and the revolution of the internet now lead to an interconnected global village, mirroring something like a Global Mind which is emerging in the realm of consciousness.

♀   **Venus**

The Venus archetype manifests through our yearnings to love and be loved, to enjoy ourselves and bring pleasure to others, and to reach out in friendship and connection. Ruling the power of attraction, our aesthetic taste and sensuality, it suggests our capacity to act in more graceful and harmonious ways with the world around us. Venus' less helpful features, such as shallowness, self-indulgence, and laziness, can perhaps be seen as created by divine consciousness itself, in order to slow down the process of spiritual breakthrough—in various ways sweetening material life and dulling the hard-edged struggle that tends to precede inner awakening.

Venus also represents our feelings of intimacy toward the divine principle as the ultimate *Beloved*, and the potential for ecstatic union with it as we regain our lost wholeness. Venus symbolizes those features of the Universal Mind which allure us toward spiritual opening with scenes of beauty and pleasure—including the sweet euphoria of romantic love, the entrancing beauty of un-spoiled nature, or the harmonious working together of all things. At this level, Venus charms us out of our attachments to the banal and everyday layers of reality, drawing us up toward higher Beauty and higher Love.

From the transpersonal side, we can see the Venus archetype in some of the motivations which the mystics attribute to Absolute Consciousness' creation of the world. These include an overwhelming love that it wants to share with other beings, and the brilliance of a connoisseur artist, savoring the universe it creates as the ultimate masterwork. Venus' loving scenes in human life, just as in the great romantic movies, have a special entertainment value in the cosmic game.

♂   **Mars**

The Mars archetype is behind our biological urges to take action and assert ourselves, to go out and participate in life, gratify our material and sexual needs, and protect ourselves during times of threat. It underlies our drives to pursue the things we want, and to actively avoid the things and experiences we don't want. The negative qualities related to Mars, such as aggression, competition, and rash actions, present many problems in the spiritual quest, tying up our attention in cycles of hurt and revenge, and delaying the healing process.

At times, old-style religious texts even seem to encourage sectarian aggression, with terrible consequences for everyone involved. In holotropic states, by contrast, people learn to withdraw their aggressive energies from the social sphere and aim them at transcendence, represented in the physical world as the space above one's head. Once the commitment of full expression without acting out is made, clients in sessions are able to express and release enormous amounts of aggression from their psyches, consuming it from a finite pool inside them and decreasing its effects in their everyday lives.

From the transpersonal side, we might suggest that Mars represents the Universal Mind's own urges toward action and adventure, one of the possible motivations for its creation of the material universe. Grof writes in *The Cosmic Game* that if we are indeed made in God's image, as we are told, then it is possible that the divine principle enjoys some of the same action and martial themes that we do as moviegoers. And if we are no more ultimately real to the divine than the characters in a film are to us, it becomes more plausible how it might enjoy or at least tolerate a certain amount of aggression in human history, as well as throughout the animal kingdom. Perhaps the Universal Mind enjoys human conflict as a kind of thickening of the plot—as we do in action movies—while leaving us the ongoing option of transcending those archaic patterns of aggression and moving closer to our spiritual nature.

♃   **Jupiter**

The Jupiter archetype manifests through our impulses to grow, reach out and expand our range of experience, to embrace wider perspectives, and to integrate ourselves into more inclusive wholes. Study, travel, and deep self-exploration are some of the fun and satisfying ways to meet these needs and broaden our horizons. This archetype also underlies feelings of optimism, joy, and well-being, our sense of adequate resources, and our impulses to generously share with our fellow human beings. Jupiter represents those forces that seek to elevate, amplify and make things bigger, leading us to pursue success and accomplishment in whatever areas of life that we consider important.

Spiritually, Jupiter suggests our impulses to move closer to, or become more like, what we consider to be true and right. It is behind our sense of the divine as being better than ourselves, as superior and existing on a higher level, and as having the capacity to uplift, improve, and make us whole. Jupiter's expansive nature seeks to draw our awareness back toward an identification with the larger universe and a more inclusive understanding of our cosmic status within it. Partial or unintegrated contact with Jupiter's expansive energy can also lead to the less salutary traits of arrogance, inflation, and excess. Material ambition is a kind of horizontal or lateral expression of Jupiter, while the heart of this archetype is toward an expansion of consciousness toward the Universal Mind and all things within it.

From the transpersonal side, we might suggest that Jupiter represents the capacity of Absolute Consciousness to add the dimension of size to its creations, unveiling universes of incredible grandeur, complexity, and magnitude. The Jupiterian features of the world have the potential to evoke awe and amazement, as we gaze out across sweeping natural landscapes or up at the deep night sky and ponder the vastness of the universe, which cosmologists now suggest may be only one of many.

♄ Saturn

The archetypal complex related to Saturn governs the small "r" reality principle, bringing order, structure, and consistency to human life. It also represents the inevitable sorrows and challenges of material incarnation. Reminding us of the birth process and our vulnerable mortality, Saturn underlies our fearful tendencies to armor and defend ourselves from past and future pain, with a consequent hardening, tightening, and limiting effect on our psyches.

The struggles associated with Saturn also lead to many positive human traits, however, including responsibility and integrity, grounded humility, hard work, and patience. Spiritual opening seems to demand that we face our limits and experience the ego reduced to a meaningless speck which then, paradoxically, allows us to reawaken to the Universal Mind and Cosmic Consciousness. During major transits of Saturn, we are more likely to feel the humbling and painful, but necessary parts of this process.

Spiritually, Saturn represents our sense of the divine as strict, judging and punishing, as keeping score, and as exacting retribution for our disobedience and mistakes. It manifests through our cautious needs to obey and toe the line, to act with utmost care and responsibility and, above all, not to hurt anyone. In one of Saturn's most extreme forms, when we are reliving the "no exit" stage of birth (Grof's Basic Perinatal Matrix II), as Tarnas recognized, we may see the universe as a soulless machine, cardboard facade, or inhuman torture chamber. In this challenging state, people selectively see the worst aspects of human existence: a terrible litany of unending wars, genocides, famines, plagues, droughts, and ecological catastrophes. In more everyday forms, people may be unable to recognize any kind of higher awareness outside of the human brain. Or they may perceive a universal consciousness but see it as unreachably remote and separate.

From the divine side, the Saturn archetype underlies the process of *involution*, as Absolute Consciousness incarnates its own being as the very substance of the material world. Saturn symbolizes the contraction and slowing down of cosmic energy into states of linear time and matter—to become the elements of the periodic table, the apparent solidity of molecules, and the boundaries around cells which make all life possible. The Saturn principle is at the root of all apparent separateness in the world. Although this limiting and defining process is essential in the act of creation, the loss of the unitive state leads to profound feelings of pain in the separate beings which are created and a deep longing to regain their lost wholeness.

A question which many seekers eventually ask during the spiritual quest is: Why does Absolute Consciousness incarnate itself into matter in the first place? If the eternal and infinite state is so wonderful, why ever seek a change? According to some mystics, the Saturn archetype may represent the sense of loneliness, monotony, or even boredom of the divine principle itself, and its impulses to create self-aware beings out of itself, with whom it can interact and relate—one of the important motives for its creation of the material world.

Saturn also represents the needs of the cosmic creative principle to initiate the laws of cause and effect, both in the physical and ethical realms. Saturn oversees the balancing and healing effect of karma in successive lifetimes, so that we have an opportunity to learn from our mistakes, strive to do better, and know what it feels like to exist on all sides of life.

♅   **Uranus**

The Uranus archetype manifests through the inner and outer forces which excite and inspire us, awakening and freeing our authentic true nature. It represents our needs for independence and individuation, our yearnings to move beyond the limits of past patterns, outmoded tradition, and fear-based pragmatism. Uranus expresses itself through the many openings and opportunities in life, unexpected resolution of problems, and the ongoing technological advancement of humanity. Evoking feelings of universal brotherhood and sisterhood, it also helps us to access a sense of planetary citizenship as we see through and transcend our differences.

The Uranus archetype's more problematic features, including manic and erratic behavior, inabilities to cooperate or compromise, and unproductive anarchism, can be seen as partial, but not fully realized contact with Uranus' freedom-seeking energies. Tarnas understood that the final stage of birth, including the crowning and completed delivery (a core element in Grof's Basic Perinatal Matrix IV), is an important manifestation of the Uranus archetype and becomes the prototype for feelings of genuine success, breakthrough, and freedom in human life. Uranus corresponds to those sides of Absolute Consciousness which allow or help us to free ourselves from the unawakened state—breakthroughs which sometimes happen unexpectedly through divine grace, as in the *satori* moment or experiences of rebirth. It signifies our sense of the divine as an eternally fresh and renewing force in human life.

From the transpersonal side, we can say that the Uranus archetype represents the Universal Mind's own excitement in the act of creation—a process in which it submerges parts of itself into material form as separate units of consciousness which forget their true origin—followed by ecstatic reawakening as those beings die or attain ego death and transcendence.

ψ   Neptune

Neptune corresponds to the *Ultimate Reality* principle, the divine source itself and our deepest yearnings to reconnect with it, remember where we came from and where we are going. Neptune transits can help us to regain states of blissful unity, satisfaction, and higher meaning. Blessedly re-enchanting our awareness through dreams and imagination, the Neptune archetype dissolves boundaries, enabling us to compassionately identify with the experiences of other people and other life forms, surrender our limiting egos, and reconnect with our true divine identity. Tarnas realized that the fetus' experience in the womb—a key element of Grof's Basic Perinatal Matrix I—is an important manifestation of Neptune and provides a template for feelings of peace, security, and connection in human life.

The Neptune archetype underlies the spiritual drive per se, the pull of our psyches to merge with divine consciousness, as well as representing the divine itself, the unbroken field of self-aware consciousness underlying all things. At the highest levels of Neptunian experience, people realize that they are not human beings having a spiritual experience, but one spiritual Superconsciousness having all the experiences. Neptune's challenging features, including vulnerability, confusion, deception, and escapism, can be seen as partial but unintegrated contact with Neptune's boundary-dissolving nature.

The ongoing question for the cosmic creative principle seems to be, at any point, deciding how much of itself to reveal. If every being in the universe were to suddenly awaken and realize their true spiritual identities, most of the countless interesting dramas of material incarnation would instantly cease—as fear, aggression, and competition disappeared. The cosmic creative principle retains this one great gift to bestow on human beings: allowing us to reawaken to our cosmic status, beyond death and separation.

♀ # Pluto

The archetypal complex related to Pluto is behind the evolutionary forces of breakdown, renewal and regeneration in the universe, manifesting as our impulses to heal and transform ourselves and the world around us. Whereas Saturn signifies death and dying, Pluto represents death and *rebirth*, subsuming the final endings associated with Saturn in the compelling creation of new life and new forms. Tarnas recognized that the dynamic stage of birth labor, with the propulsion down the birth canal and arousal of intense driving energies, is an important manifestation of the Pluto archetype in human life.

Pluto represents our struggle to confront and transform the shadow side of our psyches, which for many people involves working through leftover physical and emotional traumas—such as events in childhood or the life-threatening experience of birth with its deep imprint of human vulnerability and mortality. To the individual ego, Pluto's effects can feel ruthless and brutal. However, like the overwhelming contracting forces of the mother's delivering body, they are a necessary part of a profoundly liberating process. It is important that we face and allow Pluto's powerful energies to be expressed from our systems in supportive healing sessions, rather than acting them out harmfully in the social world.

From the transpersonal side, we could speculate that Pluto, as well as certain features of the Mars and Saturn archetypes, represent aspects of shadow within Absolute Consciousness itself, what Grof calls *Cosmic Shadow*. These negative and destructive forces deliberately set in motion during the creation of the universe seem to be a necessary component in the cosmic game, helping to keep it interesting. Without the dynamic and ever-changing energies associated with Pluto, the physical universe—like Absolute Consciousness itself—would remain eternally static, unchanging, and predictable.

The Ascendant and Descendant
Persona, Self-Expression, and Relationship

The zodiac sign that was rising on the eastern horizon when you were born is called your *rising sign* or *ascendant*. Planets aligned with your ascendant, as well as your ascendant sign, reveal your basic style of self-expression and how you relate to other people. It tends to be what people see first in you, your appearance and de-meanor, your "display window"—which is not always the same as how you actually feel inside, behind the mask of your persona. A well-integrated ascendant allows you to express your true self with consistency, integrity, and confidence, whereas a disowned or overcompensated ascendant may cause you to sell yourself short or put on a face that is not really you.

Your *descendant* is exactly opposite your ascendant and forms a dynamic polari-ty with it, the ascendant-descendant axis. Whereas the ascendant is a point of self-hood, the descendant represents your experience of other people. It describes what you seek in a relationship, qualities which you do not experience strongly in your own being but hope to discover through your partner, in order to make your psyche more whole and complete. Ultimately, these are qualities you must integrate within yourself.

Beyond Gendered Greco-Roman Planetary Names

The rebirth and revaluation of the Feminine principle in human society is one of the great overarching processes of our time. In the field of astrology, an important development in this ecstatic reawakening is the discovery of millions of new asteroids, some of which have been correlated with goddesses of Greek mythology. Their inclusion in the traditionally masculine astrological pantheon reflects a dramatic shift in how modern astrologers are making space for and reintegrating these empowering Feminine archetypes.

This is a profoundly positive direction and an important pathway for reintegrating the Feminine, yet there are other developments in the field which also reflect this dramatic Feminine rebirth and reawakening, without necessarily bringing in new celestial bodies. The central issue is that the Feminine principle, in the abundance of her many rich variations and phases, needs to be seated equally at the highest head table of the gods and goddesses. Astronomically, the asteroids are a secondary category of celestial body in relation to the planets. It follows that settling for a correlation of feminine archetypes with asteroids represents, in some ways, a marginalization of the Female principle.

Furthermore, since asteroids are relatively newly discovered celestial bodies, it is possible that some of them may have been given inaccurate names and thus characterizations. We know now that planets can be misnamed. The astrological qualities related to Neptune—peaceful, mystical, spiritual, idealistic, and imaginative—bear little resemblance to the vengeful storm-god Poseidon-Neptune in Greco-Roman mythology. Richard Tarnas recognized that the archetypal meanings related to Uranus—urges toward freedom, individuation, breakthroughs, rebellion, and change—do not match the Greek sky-god Ouranos, who was essentially a static, patriarchal figure who sought to prevent change. He suggests in *Prometheus the Awakener* that a closer parallel with the planet Uranus is the Greek titan Prometheus. In *Planets in Transit*, Rob Hand writes that a more accurate corollary with the planet Pluto is the Hindu god Shiva.

If major planets such as Uranus, Neptune, and even Pluto were poorly named or even misnamed, it is conceivable that some of the asteroids familiar to us in astrology might also be inaccurately characterized. As it was with the planets, it may take several generations of systematic observation by the worldwide community of astrologers to fully confirm, or possibly in some cases to modify, the asteroid-mythology correlations. Rather than wait for time to evaluate and confirm the asteroid meanings, there is a pressing, urgent need to make fair and equal space for the Feminine in the present astrological world. One of the most important ways we can do this is to recognize the already existing dual nature of planetary archetypes.

Every planetary archetype embodies both feminine and masculine qualities, as they are not inherently gendered and have a capacity to move between gendered manifestations. For example, the Sun, which is usually seen to embody masculine meanings, is represented by a number of goddesses around the world, including *Amaterasu* in the Japanese Shinto religion, *Sunna* in Norse mythology, and *Hashi* in the Choctaw culture of North America. The Moon, often correlated with feminine meanings, is associated with male deities such as the Sumerian *Nannar*, the Egyptian *Yah*, and Shinto *Tsukiyomi*. In the modern Ger-man language, the sun is considered to be feminine (*die* Sonne), while the Moon is masculine (*der* Mond).

Thus, the real, deeper problem is that so many of our planets were given masculine names—reflecting the masculine bias of Greco-Roman and Western culture—rather than that they are essentially masculine in nature. I suggest below some additional mythological and spiritual corollaries of the planets, in order to stimulate further thought. While I do not expect that the planets' names will be changed in the near future, I believe that students should be aware of these additional core meanings of the planetary archetypes.

The Planets and Their Feminine-Masculine Mythological Correlates

Sun	Apollo-Atman (Amaterasu)
Moon	Demeter-Isis (Parvati, Nannar)
Mercury	Mercury-Metis
Venus	Venus-Adonis (Narcissus)
Mars	Mars-Athena
Jupiter	Lakshmi-Jupiter
Saturn	Saturn-Maya (Moirai)
Uranus	Persephone-Prometheus
Neptune	Samadhi-Muses (Brahman, Tao)
Pluto	Kali-Shiva

In practice, I think it is probable that various facets of the archetypal Feminine may be represented on a number of astrological levels at the same time. For example, the mythological Hera (Roman Juno)—who embodies relationship structure and commitment, justice, equality, patience, jealousy, and insecurity—seems to correspond to alignments of Moon-Saturn, as well as to the asteroid Juno and the zodiac signs Capricorn, Cancer, and Libra, in various ways.

The mother goddess Demeter (Roman Ceres)—who embodies maternal nurture, kindness and protection, earthy abundance and fertility, and death-rebirth experiences in family relationships—is associated with Moon-Jupiter and Moon-Pluto aspects, as well as with the asteroid Ceres and the signs Virgo, Cancer, and Scorpio. These multiple, overlapping fields of meaning seem to be intrinsic to the field of cosmic consciousness, which enables a rich syncretism and pluralism in the study of the heavens.

Perceiving the Planetary Archetypes in Great Quotations

Great quotations convey the archetypes in the writer's birth chart in a highly distilled way. Johann Wolfgang von Goethe, born with Sun square Pluto, wrote, "There is strong shadow where there is much light." The Sun in astrology represents light, while Pluto corresponds to the dark or shadow elements in the psyche, and Goethe seems to be saying that these elements are combined in his experience. Tallulah Bankhead, born with Sun trine Pluto, conveyed a similar sentiment as, "I am as pure as the driven slush." Katherine Mansfield wrote the profound words, "If you wish to live, you must first attend your own funeral." She was born with the Moon at the midpoint of Uranus and Pluto (MO=UR/PL), which blends the emotional life represented by the Moon, with the psychological ego death of Pluto and the rebirth of Uranus.

William Wordsworth's (Moon-Neptune trine Uranus) evocative musing, "It is a beauteous evening, calm and free" poetically expresses the sense of lovely evening related to the Moon archetype, blended with the peaceful calm of Neptune and the freedom of Uranus. And finally, in Alfred de Musset's (born with Jupiter opposition Uranus, and Saturn semisextile Uranus): "How glorious it is—and how painful also—to be an exception" we can see Uranus' feelings of gifted uniqueness, along with Jupiter's glory and Saturn's pain.

V

Issues in Psychedelic Therapy and Self-Exploration
(from *The Astrology of Love and Relationships* and *Pathways to Wholeness*)

On Being a Good Sitter - Grof® Breathwork and Holotropic Breathwork®

The breathwork technique developed by Stan and Christina Grof has deep roots in *pranayama* from the Indian subcontinent, as well as Western experiential modalities such as Rebirthing, Primal Therapy, Reichian, and neo-Reichian approaches. The Grofs experimented with a number of processes, finally arriving at a combination of deep and rapid breathing, evocative music, focused bodywork, and mandala drawing. They also observed healing results from supportive physical contact with people suffering from emotional deprivation in infancy or childhood—resembling the "emotional corrective experiences" or "reparenting" of the best of Western psychotherapy.

Grofian approaches to breathwork are a powerful way to explore the contents of the deep unconscious, in a supportive group setting. As we have seen, holotropic states have played a fundamental role in the spiritual lives, healing practices, and rites of passage of most non-Western and preindustrial cultures for thousands of years. Many people who experience holotropic and psychedelic states for themselves develop a conviction that reintroducing these avenues for personal and collective healing is one of the most important steps we might take for our continued evolution and survival as a species. We can maintain the benefits that science and technology have given to us, while also working to re-explore and transform the disowned layers of the psyche which are creating so many urgent problems for humankind.

Workshops begin with an introductory talk on the range of possible experiences, what Grof calls "the expanded cartography of the human psyche." Participants then each choose a partner for the day. Before lunch one person "breathes" while the other "sits," and after lunch they trade places. The breather lies down with eyes closed, and when the music starts, they begin to breathe deeply and rapidly, with the process lasting usually two and a half to three hours. The idea is to let go and allow whatever is coming up to emerge into consciousness and be fully experienced. Simply breathing more deeply and rapidly than usual can activate unresolved material in the psyche, enabling it to surface for processing. Some sessions also lead to profound spiritual openings, which can take many cultural forms, relatively independent of the breather's background or culture of origin. Grof writes that the basic direction of all effective psychotherapy is to open or widen the pathway to divine consciousness.

The sitter's job is to remind the breather to maintain the faster breathing if requested, pass kleenex and water, and help them to the bathroom door when needed. Sitters quietly support the breather's process without directing or analyzing it. They trust the breather's own innate, self-healing intelligence to select the material which is most relevant for the breather, for that session. The workshop facilitators attend to the music, offer support when needed, ensure that participants complete their material and resolve in a good emotional place, and oversee a sharing circle at the end of the day.

Sitting is thus an important model for supportive relating in everyday life. Rather than the ongoing manipulation and power struggle which characterize many relationships, a more helpful approach is to acknowledge each other's wounds, as well as healthy qualities, at the outset and mutually support the healing process. Many people are hard on each other because, deep down, they are trying to remind their partner that they have more emotional processing to face. It is simply easier to respect and support people who are doing their share of the inner work.

There are few things more rewarding than watching someone we care about facing and overcoming an old pattern—like witnessing a natural birth or a peaceful death. Deep inner transformation, which involves the death of an old self and birth of a new self, can be intense and demanding but is among the greatest miracles on earth.

Issues in Psychedelic-Assisted Psychotherapy

There are a number of important issues in psychedelic-assisted psychotherapy and self-exploration that we should address. Of all the techniques for entering holotropic states of consciousness, the ingestion of psychoactive substances is undoubtedly the most powerful and controversial. Much of the debate around their use began in the late 1960s during the period of what became known as the "drug hysteria," when many young people were experimenting with psychedelics for the first time in an atmosphere of grandiose expectations and lack of experienced supervision. Sensationalist reporting of some tragic suicides and the exaggerated response of the authorities led to a blanket prohibition against not only the recreational use by young people, but the legitimate clinical programs as well. In retrospect, Grof suggests, to evaluate these powerful substances under the chaotic conditions of the 1960s was like determining that matches are inherently dangerous because children might play with them.

For many decades the opportunities for clinical research have been very poor. Fortunately, this situation has shown some dramatic improvements in the past few years. The work of the *Multidisciplinary Association for Psychedelic Studies* and other professional groups and churches has helped to create a more favorable atmosphere in the academic world, and a growing number of universities in Europe and North America have resumed their therapeutic research projects. There is also a dramatic surge of private companies conducting research. This includes promising work in the treatment of military veterans suffering from post-traumatic stress disorder (PTSD), along with treatment for depression and many other psychological conditions. As well, the almost universal experimentation with psychedelics among young people has over time evolved a somewhat more mature ethic around their use.

It is in this climate of renewed openness that I hope this book can make a contribution. Psychedelics are very powerful substances that need to be approached with utmost care and responsibility. In many ways, the ideal situation would be healthcare-funded healing centers open and available to the public, staffed by dedicated nurses, counselors, and therapists. In the absence of such programs, I am not encouraging or condoning people to rush out and take illegal drugs, especially those with a history of severe emotional problems or mental illness, or who have serious medical conditions.

The purpose of this book is to help those who have already chosen to use psychedelic substances to do so in the safest way possible, by taking care of themselves, preparing ahead, and minimizing the risks. There is a great need for more informed debate around these issues. Like many observers in this field, I also hope that legislators and administrators will inform themselves by reading the professional and scientific journals rather than the doubtful reports of sensation-hunting journalists.

What follows is a brief review of some of the most important issues and misunderstandings in this field.

Non-Specific Amplifiers of Mental Processes

According to Grof, most psychedelic substances can be understood as *non-specific amplifiers* of psychological processes. They appear to complete chemical and neural circuits in the brain that are usually interrupted—filling in the antenna so that emotional material which is normally inaccessible, can now flood into consciousness. Thus, the content of people's experiences does not come from the drug per se, but from the psyches of the journeyers themselves.

Thus, ten people ingesting LSD or psilocybin mushrooms on the same day will have ten different, sometimes even diametrically opposite, experiences. As well, one person undertaking a series of ten sessions spread out on different days might have ten different experiences. These properties of individuality and variability of experience is why it became important to find an effective predictive technique. Before Tarnas and Grof explored the diagnostic capacity of archetypal astrology, therapists had no way to predict when someone might, for example, suddenly encounter deeper and more difficult material that could require special levels of support.

The Level of Trust and Support

Whether the ingestion of a psychedelic substance ultimately becomes a positive or a negative experience depends on several major factors. The most important of these is the *level of trust* between journeyers and the people around them—their friends, guides, and sitters. As difficult material begins to surface, the journeyers' assessment of the overall safety of the situation, and the possible reactions of the people nearby, will determine whether they fully let go and face the material or desperately hold on and try to repress it. Unfortunately, the act of repressing emotional material that is trying to surface can keep it stuck in a halfway, undigested position in the psyche for days, weeks, or even years afterward.

This is the situation that many young people find themselves in, as they are being admitted to the emergency rooms of hospitals, and why psychedelic substances have acquired such a generally poor reputation in the medical community. At this critical moment in someone's life, the availability of encouraging, non-repressive support from the on-duty staff could, in many cases, quickly resolve the emerging material, change the individual's life for the better, and send him or her in a positive direction.

Similarly, patients admitted with sudden-onset emotional symptoms, such as those undergoing a psychospiritual crisis or *spiritual emergency*, if given an opportunity to simply lie down and do some deep breathing under the care of trained therapists, could have significant emotional breakthroughs and be, as one researcher put it, laughing about their experiences over dinner as opposed to entering a lifetime of damaging stigma and suppressive medication.

Set and Setting

The *setting* is the physical space where people undergo their sessions. Individuals who have adopted an internalized, therapeutic approach do their sessions in a soundproof space, ideally with beautiful scenery nearby. Those participating in the deep-indigenous traditions often perform their ceremonies in a sacred lodge or out in nature. Spiritually minded adults tend to seek out a beautiful natural setting, an intentional dance event, or an outdoor music festival; whereas many young people have their first psychedelic experience at a concert or a party, surrounded by friends, acquaintances, and sometimes by large groups of people they don't know.

Grof also discusses the various kinds of intention or *set* that participants adopt before going into their sessions and the agreements they make with other people involved in the experience. Seekers with an *internalized set* undergo sessions in order to safely activate the energies and emotions in their unconscious and face whatever comes up. The goal is to surrender deeply to the material regardless of the content and give it full verbal and physical expression. Working through leftover material is observed to be healing in two ways: by reducing the amount of emotional and energetic charge in the psyche, and by widening the pathway to ecstatic transpersonal states that have a meta-healing value.

People undergoing internalized sessions of this type are supported by at least one experienced sitter who is not under the influence of any substance. However, a male-female *dyad* is optimum. The participant agrees to remain in the reclining position with eyeshades and headphones on for the duration of the experience. During LSD sessions, this would be at least five to six hours, and for psilocybin mushroom sessions, at least three hours. Grof makes a further distinction between a *psychedelic set*, in which individuals do a single overwhelming dose of LSD or other psychedelic substance in order to reach transcendent experiences, and a *psycholytic set*, in which they do smaller doses in a series, as an adjunct to traditional psychotherapy.

Explorers approaching sessions with a *mystical set* have an intention to enter mystical states of awareness, emotionally and spiritually bond with their friends, and connect more deeply with nature. Challenging emotional material is seen as being an occasional byproduct of the process, but it is not sought out, and there are generally unspoken limits on the range of emotions that a person would be supported in facing.

The term *recreational set* applies to the act of ingesting psychedelics at a concert, a party, or other social event where the goal is to have a fun and interesting experience, essentially something out of the ordinary. Obviously, this kind of set is not conducive for facing deep emotional material and some unfortunate young people may find themselves in a situation where the intensity of their emotional process falls outside the range of acceptability for that environment. And finally, anyone familiar with the powerful effects of psychedelic substances would not hesitate to use the term *criminal set* to describe the administration of any substance to someone without their knowledge.

In practice, sessions undergone with internalized, mystical, or recreational sets can, under certain conditions, have degrees of overlap. Some young people experimenting with psychedelics at a concert or party do manage to have a genuine transcendent experience, which then persuades them to seek out a more conducive place for their next encounter. More reliably, the widespread *intentional dance venues* featuring world-music DJs create a fairly supportive setting for journeyers approaching sessions with both recreational and mystical frames of mind. (However, as always, people with a history of severe emotional problems should be careful before doing any kind of psychedelic outside of an inpatient setting.) Intentional dance events tend to attract many experienced and mature explorers. Along with healthy snacks, fresh fruit and herbal teas, the best of these events also offer a *safe room* or *chill room* with designated guides on hand to support people who are struggling and need a comforting presence.

A simple addition to this format, a *process room*, would offer an even higher degree of support. This would be a separate, enclosed space staffed by two or three experienced sitters comfortable with the full range of perinatal and transpersonal material. At least one of these sitters should be female. Anyone who felt the need would be free to come in, lie down, and give full expression to whatever was emerging in their process. For some participants, this might take hours, while for others just a few minutes. As soon as they felt good again, they could then rejoin their friends on the dance floor or in the relaxation spaces.

As the powerful evolutionary wave corresponding to our current Uranus-square-Pluto world transit moves through 2020 and beyond—which we will explore later—it is highly probable that many people will have intensified levels of emotional experience, making these kinds of processing spaces more and more crucial. The addition of a supportive sanctuary within an already safe event-space would be a small step toward recreating the miracle of the Eleusinian Mysteries in ancient Greece. As Grof writes, the role that these deeply established spiritual psychedelic rituals played in the formation of Greek culture, and thus the entire Western civilization, is yet to be fully acknowledged.

Ceremonies in the *deep indigenous tradition*, especially those originating in the Amazon areas of Brazil and Peru, represent another wave of exploration opportunities that are now available to people in many parts of the world. The number of journeyers in these powerful rituals ranges from one or two up to several dozen and thus have various degrees of mystical and internalized sets. In general, the higher the ratio of shaman and assistants to journeyers, and the more permission there is for full verbal expression, the more safe and conducive the event will be for deep processing.

The Dosage, Quality, and Purity of Psychoactive Substances

Inexperienced journeyers tend to attribute the character of their experiences to the quality of the drug or plant that they have ingested. If they have a good experience, they attribute it to the "good stuff" and if they have a bad experience, to "bad stuff." However, the *quality* of a psychedelic substance, and even the type of substance used, is much less important than most people realize. Significantly more important factors that determine the content of people's sessions include the set and setting they employ, the level of trust they have with their friends and guides, and their astrological transits.

Similarly, certain highly motivated individuals, believing that the greater the *dosage* they take, the more intense and liberating their experience will be, may ingest large doses of psychedelics under less-than-ideal circumstances. It is not uncommon to see young people who have already encountered more perinatal material than they could digest. Although, in principle, more intense journeys are likely with higher dosages, it is again people's sense of safety, their level of inner resistance, and their transits that will ultimately determine the depth of their experiences.

Grof and his colleagues observed that patients with extreme obsessive-compulsive symptomatology could, for a number of initial sessions, ingest high doses of LSD without demonstrating any change in consciousness. In one example, they administered 1000 micrograms of LSD intramuscularly to one of their severely obsessive-compulsive patients in the psychedelic program who had felt no effect from the LSD in a number of previous instances. After several hours, the young man yawned, sat up and was considered sufficiently lucid to go into the kitchen and cut bread for a snack. Conversely, people with a basic openness to their emotional process and under the influence of powerful Uranus, Neptune, or Pluto transits can enter deep holotropic states after inhaling only a small amount of marijuana, after a few minutes of deep breathing, or even spontaneously—as in the case of those undergoing a spiritual emergency. It should be noted that the *threshold dosage* of LSD for human beings is between 300–500 micrograms. Beyond this level, there are no further chemical effects on the brain or changes in consciousness (Grof, 2008).

And finally, the *purity* of psychoactive compounds is obviously very important. Most LSD that is available in the West at the present time is apparently chemically pure and seems to be rarely handled by the more unscrupulous criminal elements. Psilocybin mushrooms are either the real thing or completely fake, although there is always the possibility that an unknown source could add something foreign to them. Similarly, it is very unlikely that individuals ingesting ayahuasca, ibogaine, or other natural plant medicines will encounter anything less than pure versions of these compounds. It is MDMA, or ecstasy, that has the highest potential for batches adulterated with other substances. This is for two main reasons: first, because its typical powdered form is easy to tamper with, and second, because it is one of the most desirable party drugs for naive and unquestioning young people.

Another important issue is the possible side effects of the *pure* form of psychoactive substances themselves. Clinical researchers after more than five decades of *in vitro* and *in vivo* testing have been unable to find biological side effects of pure LSD. Effective in incredibly minute quantities—millionths of a gram—the lysergic acid molecules are broken down into their constituent parts and secreted into the urine stream within two hours after ingestion. What are known as "flashback" effects are not caused by chemical residues left in the body, but from unprocessed emotions from the unconscious that were activated but not fully worked through. Psilocybin mushrooms and ayahuasca also have no significant toxin by-products.

It is with ecstasy, again, because of its amphetamine content that due care and diligence needs to be observed. All amphetamine-based drugs can cause problems for people with pre-existing heart conditions or hypertension. Ecstasy can also lead to dehydration, or hyperthermia, in warm environments if people do not drink enough water—or to low blood sodium levels, or hyponatremia, from drinking too much water, a problem which can be easily corrected by ingesting salt or electrolytes during the evening. Research into other effects from prolonged high-dose exposure to ecstasy, such as possible change in the neurons that make serotonin in the brain, has yielded mixed results and at this point seems inconclusive, with the effects almost certainly less serious or permanent than originally believed. It should be noted that most of the fatalities associated with ecstasy have occurred when it was combined with other, medicinal, drugs such as monoamine oxidase inhibitors (MAO Inhibitors).

Medical and Psychiatric Contraindications for Holotropic States

Holotropic states can, at times, involve highly strenuous emotional and energetically charged material, and therefore people approaching them need to be aware of certain medical and psychiatric contraindications. The most important contraindications of a medical nature include cardiovascular disease and high blood pressure, brain hemorrhage, aneurysms, myocarditis, or atrial fibrillation—and the risks increase exponentially with fast-acting psychedelics such as 5-MeO-DMT. Other concerns include serious diabetes, glaucoma, retinal detachment, osteoporosis, a history of dislocations and fractures, and severe epilepsy. Not all the conditions in this second category are absolute contraindications, but people need to discuss them fully with their sitters and physicians beforehand. Individuals who have recently undergone surgery or suffered a recent injury should also be aware of the possibility of reinjuring themselves in the strenuous phases of breathwork or psychedelic therapy sessions.

Bronchial asthma is not a contraindication, but people should have their inhaler on hand and sitters need to be aware of the possibility of suffocation material from birth emerging, which, as always, can be very healing if sup-ported. And finally, pregnant women should not ingest powerful psychedelics for obvious reasons. Even Grof® Breathwork could pose a risk in the later trimesters because an activation of the mother's own perinatal material could potentially induce labor. However, Grof notes that, because of the openness of the mother's psyche, the weeks and months after delivery provide an opportunity for unusually deep inner work. Avenues for emotional processing should, ideally, be considered a standard option available to post-partum mothers. Health care providers including nurses, midwives and doulas trained in nurturing and releasing forms of breathwork could offer an invaluable additional service to the women and families in their care.

With regard to *psychiatric contraindications*, people with a history of severe emotional problems, especially those who have been hospitalized or diagnosed with mental illness, need to be very careful before considering doing any kind of psychedelic or intense breathwork. Under ideal conditions, the holotropic approach has been proven to benefit many categories of mental illness of psychogenic origin, i.e., problems that do not have a clear biological basis such as those caused by brain tumours or fevers (Grof, 2008). However, patients with a history of serious psychological problems often need extra care that extends beyond the time frame of a breathwork seminar—backup care which can only be provided by an inpatient facility. There is an urgent need for responsible therapists to begin pilot projects and create these kinds of programs.

The other psychiatric concern is that a tendency toward dangerous acting out that characterizes bipolar disorder, in particular, can present special safety and legal issues for deep work with manic individuals. The possibility that anything the person does for the rest of their life might be attributed to the emotional processing is, in our present philosophical climate, a serious obstacle to working with some of the people who need it most. An inpatient facility with twenty-four-hour supervision for the periods between sessions would, again, offer an opportunity for manic individuals to work through their driving emotional material and reach states of genuine rebirth.

The Hero or Heroine's Journey

The overall direction of the perinatal sequence is thus a descent into the underworld, a firsthand confrontation with disowned and repulsive elements of human nature, with mortality, and death, followed by a return to the dayworld of society renewed and transformed. This pattern also forms the basis of the hero or heroine's journey discovered by the mythologist Joseph Campbell. The universal spiritual pattern or *monomyth* which he describes reflects, in mythological language, the passage of the fetus as it leaves the security of the womb, descends down and through the birth canal, and then out into new life. It also mirrors the process of the adult ego facing this material.

Further, these two levels of experience—the obstetric and the archetypal—are inseparably blended in the human psyche. Thus, when journeyers access good-womb memories (Grof's BPM I), they have a sense of blissful existence, security, and belonging in a pristine cosmic realm which transcends evil and conflict. This correlates with the innocence and security of the *Ordinary World* stage in Camp-bell's monomyth. As individuals in holotropic states relive the onset of labor (BPM II), they often have images of descending into a whirlpool, maelstrom, or under-world, being engulfed inside a whale, or attacked by a giant octopus or tarantula. These painful experiences encompass Campbell's stages of *The Call to Adventure, Crossing the Threshold, Approach to the Inmost Cave,* and *The Belly of the Whale* in the hero or heroine's journey through the underworld.

When journeyers are working through material from the dynamic stage of labor (Grof's BPM III), they pass through intense episodes of death-rebirth struggle. These experiences correspond to the *Allies and Enemies, Tests and Ordeals, Tempta-tion,* and *Abyss* stages in Campbell's sequence. And finally, people who relive the moment of crowning and delivery (BPM IV) enjoy scenes of ecstatic rebirth, explo-sive liberation, and emergence into divine light. These parallel Campbell's stages of *The Gifts of the Goddess, Resurrection, Revelation, Reward, Atonement, Transformation, The Road Back, Return with Elixir,* and *Freedom to Live* in his passage of the hero or heroine's journey.

Systems of Condensed Experience (COEXes)

Grof found that when individuals involved in psychotherapy enter holotropic states, their memories do not surface randomly but tend to emerge in groups, which are bound together by a similar emotion or sensation. He calls these clusters of memory, *COEX systems*—and he views them as similar, though not identical to, Jung's concept of the psychological complexes. For Grof, the connecting element in a COEX can be either a powerful *emotion*, such as shame, ridicule, humiliation, happiness, or security; or a strong *sensation*, such as suffocation, pressure in some part of the body, or relaxed satisfaction. He also found that, during inner work, the more recent components of these memory systems tend to emerge first, beginning with episodes from people's biography, then moving deeper into material from the birth process, and finally often to transpersonal layers.

Thus, a person could relive a series of memories based on suffocation. This might include memories from postnatal life of near-drowning or attempted strangu-lation by a sibling, then deepen to experiences of suffocation during delivery, and finally to a past life or collective memory of being hanged on the gallows. Another COEX might involve memories of being rejected by one's mother, then deepen into experiences of being unwanted in utero, and finally to a past life involving murderous hate between two people. These are just several examples. Grof found that in order to heal the problems related to a particular COEX, people must be willing to face each layer of it in succession, until they reach the core experience. During the process of inner exploration, people can also discover, within their psyches, nourishing karmic patterns from what feel like past lives. This is one of the many healing mechanisms which can emerge spontaneously in transpersonal psychotherapy.

Each of us is thus influenced by clusters of positive and negative memories in our psyches, and this helps to explain why our moods and feelings can change so abruptly in everyday life. If we are under the influence of a COEX involving experiences of great suffering—such as punishment during childhood, a long and complicated birth, and a difficult past life memory—we will tend to feel anxious, depressed, unhappy, and pessimistic in our present life situation. Later on, the flashlight of awareness may switch over to a positive memory system—for example, one based on happy times in our family life, blissful womb memories, peaceful periods in our racial history, and finally to a nourishing and supportive archetype—and we will feel a sense of happiness, well-being, safety, and optimism.

Tarnas and Grof discovered that the COEX systems in a person's psyche tend to correlate with major planetary alignments in their birth chart. Thus, COEX systems involving experiences of abandonment, ridicule, or judgment are often reflected by difficult aspects involving Saturn. Further, rejection by the mother will tend to correspond to Saturn-*Moon* alignments, whereas problems with the father, to those of Saturn-*Sun*. Of course, Moon-Saturn and Sun-Saturn aspects can also indicate, for many people, a solidly enduring and dependable relationship with their mother or father.

Tarnas and Grof also observed that current *transits* to a natal aspect will tend to activate the COEX systems associated with that aspect. Thus, a person with a COEX involving abandonment and lack of nurturing, related to a natal Moon square Saturn, will tend to feel the emotions related to that COEX surface whenever a powerful transiting planet lights up their Moon-Saturn square. These will also be times when they can do the deepest work to resolve the issues related to those memories. The understanding of COEX systems and their activation by transits is a tremendous help in understanding the dynamics in people's relationships and how they change over time. In the following sections, I will explore some of the most important emotional themes which can surface in people's lives during the various planetary transits. (See the graphic on p. 80).

Relationship COEXes

I am also proposing a new term: *relationship COEX*. Relationship COEXes are groupings of both positive and negative memories which accumulate in a couple's history together. During happy periods they will tend to remember and be influenced by their many previous good experiences, with a resulting sense of ongoing love, peace, and satisfaction. In times of conflict, however, they will tend to remember negative experiences from their history, and may even bring them up for rehashing, which further fuels the conflict. Their relationship memory systems will be rooted in the COEXes of each person in the relationship, as well as new memory COEXes based on their unique chemistry and interactions together.

Relationship COEXes are reflected by the planetary alignments in a couple's synastry chart (a side-by-side comparison of their two birth charts) and composite chart (a chart based on the midpoint position of their two natal Suns, Moons, and so on), as we shall explore. At this early stage of research, the major COEXes in a relationship seem to be indicated by aspects involving the Sun or Moon, or by alignments which involve multiple planets in an aspect field, both by composite and synastry.

VI

Principles of Holotropic Dreamwork
(Partially from *The Archetypal Universe*)

Principles of Holotropic Dreamwork

As C. G. Jung and the major figures in Western depth psychology confirm, the more consciously we face the archetypal forces within us, the more friendly and supportive a relationship we will have with the totality of our psyches and with the larger universe around us. Deep self-exploration helps to transform difficult emotional energies and bring out their more positive forms.

In the holotropic approach to psychological unfolding, for example, there are no good and bad dreams. Every remembered dream is a breakthrough in consciousness, helping people to feel the emotions that are trying to surface inside them. Each part of a dream represents a part of the dreamer's own psyche. The various pleasant and painful emotions that dreams bring up are overseen by our own "inner healers," as they work to expand our psyches to embrace every emotion and every part of the greater Universal Psyche, which is our true identity.

Tarnas has referred to dreams as "nightly non-ordinary states," an idea which Grof also mentions in *LSD Psychotherapy* (1980). My research supports their view that the same principles apply to the understanding and interpretation of dreams as to that of holotropic and psychedelic experiences. Our dreams represent a mind-opening holotropic ("moving toward wholeness") process that is always working within our psyches—and directed by our inner healers—helping us to keep in balance, face our buried fears and trauma, and open our awareness to divine consciousness. As we have seen, Tarnas found that the themes and timing of these inner healing forces can be illuminated by our planetary transits. In *Pathways to Wholeness* (2014), I explore the interplay between astrological archetypes and the psychological material that emerges in holotropic and psychedelic healing sessions. This Grofian-Tarnasian model is, in my experience, an invaluable guide for understanding dreams as well.

Complementary insights into dreams can be found in the important writings of C. G. Jung and scholars in the Jungian tradition. The single most helpful and influential volume for me has been the classic *Man and His Symbols* (1968). In the following section, I explore many correlations between the approaches of Jung, Grof, and Tarnas in these areas. The most interesting parallels in their approaches to the psyche and dreamwork involve elements of character, setting, imagery, mood, and emotion: essentially, the inner-healer part of our psyches creates an ingenious story which has the same emotional and sensory qualities as the psychological material which it wants us to face. If we are working through leftover fear from early traumas, we will tend to dream of scary situations that help us to feel this repressed anxiety. If we are accessing euphoric states of spiritual transcendence, we may dream about ecstatic flying or gliding, experiences that bring these emotions into consciousness.

It is not important to mentally understand the content of our dreams. The most important thing is our willingness to slow down, remember the sequence of our dreams, and deeply feel the emotions they awaken. We need to take the time to stay immersed in their shadings of mood and emotion. We do not interpret the dream as a message about our external life, but as an invitation to remain and deepen into the realm of soul within us. James Hillman called this process "soul-making." We can also practice the work of "active imagination" described by Hillman and Jung. While remaining in the setting of a dream, we allow our imagination to unfold in whatever direction it wants to go. This tends to bring up more feelings and often moves in the direction of perinatal or archetypal imagery. We may also experientially become, through our imaginations, any part of a dream—a person, an animal, a clock on the wall—seeing the scene from their perspective and feel what they are feeling. If we do not fully understand a dream, then uncertainty is the emotion that we are supposed to feel in that moment.

Number Symbolism in Dreams

There is a more specific and limited subset of dream study that I also want to introduce now, that of number symbolism. Jung's insight into the symbolism of numbers has astonishing correlations with Grof's sequence of the perinatal matrices. In Jung's dream observations, the number *one* corresponds to experiences of unity, oneness, and primal integration of the conscious and unconscious aspects of being. This understanding bears many similarities with Grof's Basic Perinatal Matrix *I*, as well as with the archetype of *Neptune*, as Tarnas recognized. Both Neptune and BPM I encompass states of unity, transcendence of boundaries, and merging of the individual self with the Universal Self. When people dream about *one* of something, they often wake up with feelings, to various degrees, of awe, mystery, peace, serenity, and higher meaning.

The most common symbol of this type is a single body of water, such as a lake, a river, or the ocean. Other archetypes merging with Neptune will then shape its unitive, oceanic themes in more specific ways. Neptune-*Venus* transits can add qualities of beauty, romance and friendship, such as romantic cruises on a serene and peaceful ocean, or friends enjoying a relaxing swim in a special river together. Neptune-*Mars* transits tend to bring elements of energy, speed and heat to Neptunian dreams, such as people sloshing down water slides, racing on lakes, swimming with gusto, or soaking in hot springs.

In a similar way, dreamers may find themselves on the first floor—i.e., the number one—of a four-story building. Neptune can also manifest through various religious and spiritual symbols. When combined with the *Sun*, people may dream of wise spiritual teachers and gurus; with *Mercury*, of sacred chants or mantras; and with *Jupiter*, of divine Providence and positive or miraculous outcomes.

For Jung, the number *two* is a symbol of duality, opposites, and adversarial relationships, but also the increased awareness that results from the hard work to integrate the various opposites and polarities in the psyche. Comparably in the Grof-Tarnas model, Saturn and BPM *II* represent states of duality, suffering, and constriction but also the necessary submersion into ego consciousness and materiality during the process of incarnation. When people dream about two of something, which seems to happen more frequently during Saturn transits, they often gain a new sense of problems, challenges, and inner work that needs to be done.

Other archetypes interacting with Saturn will then affect the specific forms that dream images might take. During Saturn-*Moon* transits, people can dream about two family members or two small women, rejection by one's mother, entrapment in tight confining rooms, or wise elder queens; whereas Saturn-*Mercury* combinations can show up as two-wheeled bicycles, as problems with vehicles, as not knowing one's lines for a play, or as stressful exams. Saturn-*Venus* transits can manifest as two pies at a dull retirement party, as two musicians, or as romantic heartache, boring music, or old friends. Interestingly, during Saturn-*Neptune* transits, people may dream about an interplay between Saturnian states of duality and those of Neptunian unity.

In Jung's dream research, the number *three* represents an active struggle to resolve the opposing inner forces symbolized by the number two. This usually involves the need to integrate darker shadow material in order to achieve wholeness, along with a sense of evolutionary processes that are almost but not yet quite complete. In a similar way for Tarnas and Grof, Pluto and the *third* perinatal matrix represent the death-rebirth struggle to overcome the oppressive dualities of the material world and transcend the fear of death—accompanied by the catharsis of powerful energies, confrontation with deep shadow material, and a sense of moving toward, but not yet reaching transcendence. I found that dreams about three of something tend to coincide with periods of erupting emotion in people's lives, of driving forces pushing them onward, and of graphic exposure to any or all of the themes in Grof's BPM III (activation of aggressive, erotic, disgusting, morally inverted, or fiery elements).

As Tarnas' work might predict, these dreams seem to be more common during strong transits of Pluto. As in our previous examples, other archetypes interacting with Pluto will then add their unique thematic signatures. Pluto combined with the *Moon* can take the form of dreams about three women, three homes, or three children, whereas transits of Pluto-*Mars* can manifest as three cars playing a dangerous game of chicken, or as three men clad in black. Pluto-*Venus* transits can show up as three menacing dolls, while Pluto-*Mercury*, as dreams about triangle shapes— which suggest perinatal elements and the pubic triangle—or as journeys with three important stages.

And finally, Jung discovered that the number *four* appears in people's dreams when they have reached a plateau of wholeness, integration, and individuation in their evolutionary journey, and are connecting with the archetype of the Self. Incredibly, in the Grof-Tarnas sequence, Uranus and BPM *IV* also encompass states of rebirth, awakening and wholeness, reunion with divine consciousness, and biological separation from the mother during the completed delivery. When people dream about four of something, they often feel a sense of success, completion, and integration for that cycle of personal growth. During Uranus-*Moon* transits, people can dream of four-sided homes, four family members, four young people, or four bursts of emotion, whereas during Uranus-*Sun* transits, they might see four men sitting around a table with sunshine streaming in. Uranus-*Venus* alignments can manifest as four people singing, as four fun and vivacious women, or as four flowers. Uranus-*Mercury* can show up as four days of driving, while Uranus-*Pluto* as four flames.

What is so interesting is that Grof did not assign numbers to his four stages so they might fit a preconceived framework, but simply in order of the successive stages of birth—i.e., he discovered patterns that were created by the cosmic creative principle and Mother Nature herself. And yet the thematic qualities of his perinatal matrices exactly match the thematic qualities of the numbers one, two, three, and four in the dreams of Jung's patients. Thus, when individuals are influenced by memories of BPM I, they tend to have dreams about one of something. When they are working through material from BPM II, they frequently dream of two characters or two things, and so forth.

To pursue this further, the number *five*—which often conveys a sense of unnecessary egotism in the dreamer's approach to life that requires active letting go and change—seems to be thematically related to elements of both Pluto and *Mars*, which is, synchronistically, the fifth major body in the solar system. The meaning of *six*, often associated with feelings of higher integration, abundance, completeness, and evolutionary success in dreams—has a resonance with both Uranus and *Jupiter*, the *sixth* major body in the solar system. Dreams involving five or six are relatively rare, however, and more research will be needed to either confirm or modify these hypotheses.

The fascinating correlations between the research of Jung, Grof, and Tarnas are a powerful confirmation of the authenticity and universality of dream symbols, and it is clear that number symbolism is just one small part of the congruencies between them—these parallels are less surprising when we remember that Grof understands the perinatal matrices as being biological manifestations of universal archetypes. Finally, I was inspired in my dream research by the gifted writing style of James Hillman. The book that I would initially recommend to readers is *The Dream and the Underworld* (1979) followed by *Re-Visioning Psychology* (1975).

In summary, our dreams are part of a healing and awakening process that is always happening inside us, one that has been mapped and explored by some of the major figures in depth and transpersonal psychology, and especially by research into psychedelic states. Tarnas' work in archetypal astrology has added the element of time to this understanding: planetary transits help to reveal *when* a given Jungian archetype or Grofian BPM is more likely to emerge in people's dream lives. The images in our dreams are, of course, multidimensional and multivalent—they take many variable shapes and cannot be concretely predicted using astrology alone. What astrology can do is predict the archetypal *flavor* of dreams: the overall emotional tenor, broad categories of inner experience, and a range of possible themes and symbols—as well as provide an invaluable guide for dream interpretation and emotional work afterward.

I found that both people's individual transits and the current world transits will shed light on these inner motifs. The content of our dreams seems to be determined by the archetypal forces related to both our personal transits and those of the ongoing world transits, in relatively equal measure. Most of the correlations that I observed between planetary archetypes and dream elements involved quadrature alignments (conjunctions, oppositions, and squares), while only a small percentage of dreams were reflected by trine or sextile transits.

VII Weekly Sequence of Classes

Class 1

We will do a round on Zoom where everyone will have an opportunity to say hello and introduce themselves. You can briefly share your background, your interests in astrology and deep self-exploration, and what you are hoping to learn from the course.

I will also talk about the structure of the course and some ways to get the most out of it. Several of my archetypal astrology colleagues will also say hello.

If you want to, you can write down people's names here:

We will then practice drawing the astrological glyphs:

The Luminaries and Planets

Sun ☉

Moon ☽

Mercury ☿

Venus ♀

Mars ♂

Jupiter ♃

Saturn ♄

Uranus ♅

Neptune ♆

Pluto ♇

Ascendant **AC**

Midheaven **MC**

The Major Aspects

Conjunction ☌

Sextile ⚹

Square ☐

Trine △

Opposition ☍

Midpoints (a=b/c). For example, Uranus at the midpoint of Venus and Mars is written as: ♅=♀/♂.

The Signs

Aries ♈

Taurus ♉

Gemini ♊

Cancer ♋

Leo ♌

Virgo ♍

Libra ♎

Scorpio ♏

Sagittarius ♐

Capricorn ♑

Aquarius ♒

Pisces ♓

Fig. 2 From the *Archetypal Explorer* Program by Kyle Nicholas.

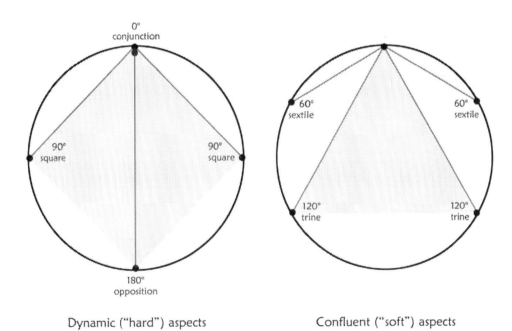

Dynamic ("hard") aspects   Confluent ("soft") aspects

Fig. 3a-b From Rick Tarnas' *Cosmos and Psyche.* Many thanks to Becca Tarnas and her excellent and recommended *Archetypal Astrology Guide* for the idea to include the above two graphics.

We will also practice spotting aspects.

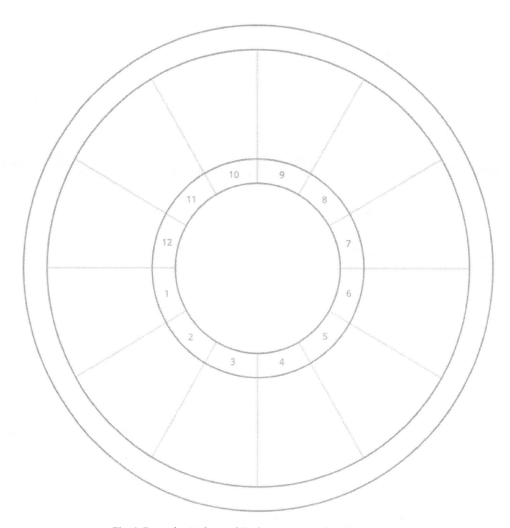

Fig. 4 From the *Archetypal Explorer* program by Kyle Nicholas.

What Aspects Do I Have?

Class 2

Grof's Expanded Cartography of the Human Psyche

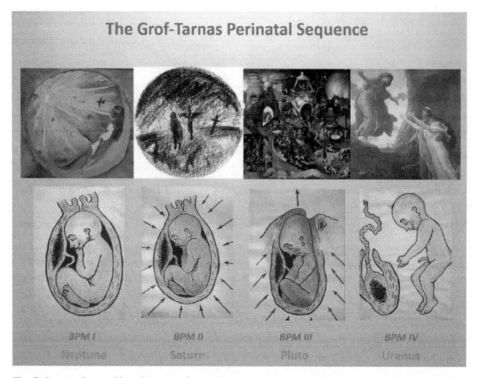

Fig. 5 During deep self-exploration, the perinatal layer of the psyche emerges in four broad bands of experience, which Grof terms the *basic perinatal matrices* or *BPMs*. Each BPM contains a mixture of obstetric, historical, karmic, archetypal, and spiritual elements. Unresolved material from this layer of the psyche is one of the deepest sources of human insatiable greed, aggression, and fear (Grof, 2008). Tarnas' correlation of the four outermost planets with Grof's perinatal matrices has deepened our understanding of planetary archetypes, by placing them in context within the natural sequence of biological birth and spiritual rebirth.

Credits: BPM I painting, "In the Lap of the Goddess," by Silvina Heath. *BPM II* drawing, "Landscape of Everlasting Pain and Loneliness," by Tauno Leinonen. *BPM III* painting, "Christ in Limbo," by a follower of Hieronymous Bosch. *BPM IV* painting, "The Return of Persephone," by Frederic Leighton.

What Was My Birth Like?

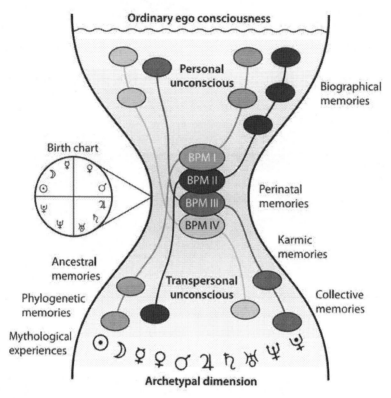

Fig. 6 Model designed by Tarnas with graphic by Darrin Drda, which depicts the structure of COEX systems in the human psyche, spanning the three layers of the unconscious: the biographical, perinatal, and transpersonal realms. It also reveals their connection through bands of memory in the unconscious, which Grof terms COEX systems. Archetypal principles inform the entire structure. During the inner archaeological quest, we can gradually explore, make conscious, and resolve these various layers of our psyches.

Tarnas writes that throughout our lives these memory COEXes "accumulate greater and greater psychic and somatic charge, like a snowball going downhill, drawing into themselves more events and experiences that magnify the inherited psychosomatic structures and impulses until they are made conscious and integrated." (From Tarnas' epilogue in *The Way of the Psychonaut*.)

What are Some of the Major Patterns of Experience in My Life and How Do They Correspond to Aspects in My Chart?

Class 3

Sun-Neptune

Core Meanings (Write in these core meanings from *The Archetypal Universe* or any other source.)

+

-

It speaks out [of]…a million eyes, it expresses itself in countless gestures, and there is no village or country road where that broad-branched tree cannot be found in whose shade the ego struggles for its own abolition, drowning the world of multiplicity in the All and All-Oneness of Universal Being.

   C. G. Jung (Sun square Neptune) *Psychology and Religion* (Referring to India)

We are spirits in the material world.

   Sting (Sun conjunct Neptune) "Spirits in the Material World"

If I could know me, I could know the universe.

   Shirley MacLaine (Sun trine Neptune) *Dancing in the Light*, 1985

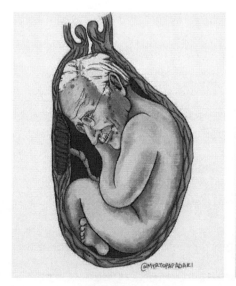 

Figs. 7-8 Art on left by Myrto Papadaki. On right by Elena Andrade.

Do I have Sun-Neptune natally?

When did I have a Neptune-to-Sun transit and what was my experience?

Some famous people who have it (add these in from my slideshows or any other source):

People in my life who have it:

Notes and Research

Fig. 9 Carl Gustav Jung

Notes and Research

Sun-Saturn

Core Meanings   +

-

You gain strength, courage and confidence by every experience in which you really stop to look fear in the face. You are able to say to yourself, "I lived through this horror. I can take the next thing that comes along."... You must do the thing you think you cannot do.

   Eleanor Roosevelt (Sun trine Saturn) *You Learn by Living*, 1960

It is not the end of the physical body that should worry us. Rather, our concern must be to live while we're alive—to release our inner selves from the spiritual death that comes with living behind a façade designed to conform to external definitions of who and what we are.

   Elisabeth Kübler-Ross (Sun-Pluto trine Saturn) *On Death and Dying*, 1969

Fig. 10 Eleanor Roosevelt

Do I have Sun-Saturn natally?

When did I have a Saturn-to-Sun transit and what was my experience?

Some famous people who have it:

People in my life who have it:

Notes and Research

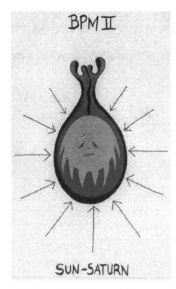

Fig. 11 Art by Mango Johnstone.

Notes and Research

Class 4

Sun-Pluto

Core Meanings   +

-

[Every ideology can be seen as] the personal confession of its author…. Psychology shall be recognized again as the queen of the sciences, for whose service and preparation the other sciences exist. For psychology is now again the path to the fundamental problems.

    Friedrich Nietzsche (Sun opposition Pluto) *Beyond Good and Evil,* 1886

There is strong shadow where there is much light.

    Johann von Goethe (Sun square Pluto) *Gotz von Berlichingen,* 1773

Fig. 12 Art by Elena Andrade.

Do I have Sun-Pluto natally?

When did I have a Pluto-to-Sun transit and what was my experience?

Some famous people who have it:

People in my life who have it:

Notes and Research

Notes and Research

Fig. 13 Stanislav Grof (born with Sun-Mercury-Jupiter-Pluto conjunction)

Sun-Uranus

Core Meanings +

-

So happy just to be alive
Underneath this sky of blue
On this new morning with you.
    Bob Dylan (Sun conjunct Uranus) "New Morning"

Life is either a daring adventure or nothing. To keep our faces toward change and be-
have like free spirits in the presence of fate is strength undefeatable.
    Helen Keller (Sun sextile Uranus) *Let Us Have Faith*, 1940

Two roads diverged in a wood, and I,
I took the one less traveled by,
And that has made all the difference.
    Robert Frost (Sun trine Uranus) "The Road Not Taken" 1916

Fig. 14-15 Photo on left, Helen Keller. Art on right by Myrto Papadaki.

Do I have Sun-Uranus natally?

When did I have a Uranus-to-Sun transit and what was my experience?

Some famous people who have it:

People in my life who have it:

Notes and Research

Figs. 16-17 Photo on left by Heather Malcolm Tarnas. Art on right by Elena Andrade.

Notes and Research

Fig. 18 Art by Eva Ursiny.

Class 5

Moon-Neptune

Core Meanings   +

-

Late on the third day, at the very moment, when, at sunset, we were making our way through a herd of hippopotamuses, there flashed upon my mind, unforeseen and un-sought, the phrase, "Reverence for Life."

   Albert Schweitzer (Moon conjunct Neptune) *Out of My Life and Thought,* 1949

My religion is kindness.

   The Dalai Lama (Moon conjunct Neptune)

 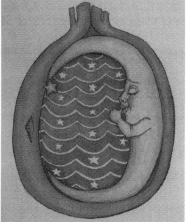

Figs. 19-20 Art on left "In the Lap of the Goddess" by Silvina Heath, from a breathwork session during a transit of Neptune conjunct her natal Moon. Art on right by Olena Provencher.

Do I have Moon-Neptune natally?

When did I have a Neptune-to-Moon transit and what was my experience?

Some famous people who have it:

People in my life who have it:

Notes and Research

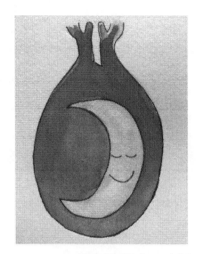 

Figs. 21-22 Art on left by Elena Andrade. Photo on right is the Dalai Lama.

Notes and Research

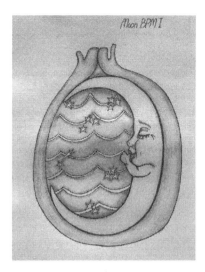

Fig. 23 Art by Olena Provencher.

Moon-Saturn

Core Meanings   +

-

You cannot make yourself feel something you do not feel, but you can make yourself do right in spite of your feelings.
  Pearl Buck (Moon sextile Saturn) *To My Daughters, With Love*, 1967

We are healed of a suffering only by experiencing it to the full.
  Marcel Proust (Moon trine Saturn) "The Sweet Cheat Gone,"
  Remembrance of Things Past

Fig. 24 Jean Paul Sartre in the "no-exit" stage of birth. In February of 1935, Sartre had a poorly managed and unresolved mescaline session which left him with acute feelings of anxiety and depression. Grof writes that Sartre's philosophy of existentialism can be seen as an expression of BPM II: the fear of death and insanity, the horror of being engulfed and trapped, the underlying feelings of loneliness, guilt, and inferiority, and a profound sense of the absurdity of life. Sartre's dominant influence during this unresolved session was transiting Saturn conjunct his natal Moon-Saturn conjunction.
  It is important to remember, however, that major figures in the history of depth psychology, such as Jung (born with Moon square Saturn) and Grof (Moon conjunct Saturn), as well as many mystics throughout the ages, were able to successfully face and pass through Saturn's dark night of the soul, and reach beyond it to the numinous transpersonal realms. Art by Olena Provencher.

Do I have Moon-Saturn natally?

When did I have a Saturn-to-Moon transit and what was my experience?

Some famous people who have it:

People in my life who have it:

Notes and Research

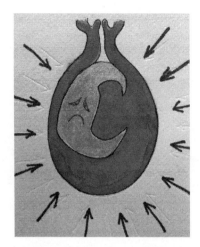

Fig. 25 Art by Elena Andrade.

Notes and Research

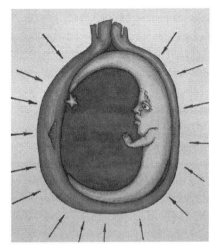

Fig. 26 Art by Olena Provencher.

Class 6

Moon-Pluto

Core Meanings   +

-

The place of magic transformation and rebirth, together with the underworld and its inhabitants, are presided over by the Mother. On the negative side, the Mother archetype may connote anything secret, hidden, dark; the abyss, the world of the dead, anything that devours, seduces and poisons, that is terrifying and inescapable like fate.

 C. G. Jung (Moon conjunct Pluto) *The Archetypes and the Collective Unconscious,* 1981

Everyone is a moon, and has a dark side which he never shows to anybody.

 Mark Twain (Moon conjunct Pluto) "Following the Equator" 1897

Only that which is deeply felt changes us.

 Marilyn Ferguson (Moon semisextile Pluto) *The Aquarian Conspiracy,* 1980

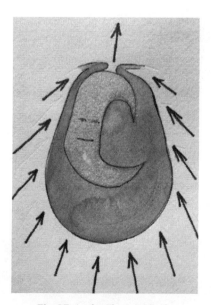

Fig. 27 Art by Elena Andrade.

Do I have Moon-Pluto natally?

When did I have a Pluto-to-Moon transit and what was my experience?

Some famous people who have it:

People in my life who have it:

Notes and Research

Notes and Research

Moon-Uranus

Core Meanings +

-

True emancipation begins neither at the polls nor in courts. It begins in woman's soul.
   Emma Goldman (Moon conjunct Uranus) *Anarchism and Other Essays,* 1911

Emotion is the chief source of all becoming-conscious. There can be no transforming of darkness into light and of apathy into movement without emotion.
   C. G. Jung (Moon square Uranus) *Psychological Aspects of the Modern Archetype,* 1938

Fig. 28 Art by Olena Provencher.

Do I have Moon-Uranus natally?

When did I have a Uranus-to-Moon transit and what was my experience?

Some famous people who have it:

People in my life who have it:

Notes and Research

Notes and Research

Fig. 29 Art by Olena Provencher.

Class 7

Mercury-Neptune

Core Meanings   +

-

I've dreamt in my life dreams that have stayed with me ever after, and changed my ideas: they've gone through and through me, like wine through water, and altered the color of my mind.

 Emily Brontë (Mercury trine Neptune) *Wuthering Heights,* 1847

Human existence is girt round with mystery; the narrow region of our experiences is a small island in the midst of a boundless sea.

 William James (Mercury semisextile Neptune) *Utility of Religion,*1874

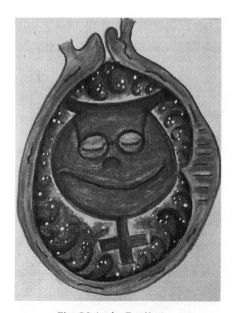

Fig. 30 Art by Eva Ursiny.

Do I have Mercury-Neptune natally?

When did I have a Neptune-to-Mercury transit and what was my experience?

Some famous people who have it:

People in my life who have it:

Notes and Research

Notes and Research

Mercury-Saturn

Core Meanings   +

-

Every man takes the limits of his own field of vision for the limits of the world.
    Arthur Schopenhauer (Mercury conjunct Saturn) *Studies in Pessimism*, 1851

All is to be doubted.
    Rene Descartes (Mercury trine Saturn) *Discourse on Method*, 1637

I'm not denyin' the women are foolish: God Almighty made 'em to match the men.
    George Eliot (Mercury square Saturn)

Fig. 31 In a replay of the fetus' experience compressed within the contracting uterine walls, Mercury's vision and perspective can be constricted by Saturn, leading to negative thinking and pessimism. However, Saturn can also help to ground and focus Mercury's thought processes, enabling a more sober, organized, and practical mental approach. Art by Eva Ursiny.

Do I have Mercury-Saturn natally?

When did I have a Saturn-to-Mercury transit and what was my experience?

Some famous people who have it:

People in my life who have it:

Notes and Research

Notes and Research

Class 8

Mercury-Pluto

Core Meanings   +

-

Miss Bart had the gift of following an undercurrent of thought while she appeared to be sailing on the surface of conversation.
   Edith Wharton (Mercury square Pluto) *The House of Mirth*, 1905

A fanatic is one who can't change his mind and won't change the subject.
   Winston Churchill (Mercury opposition Pluto)

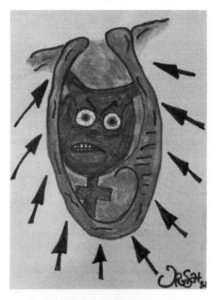

Fig. 32 Grof's research suggests that the fetus' experience of suffocation during its long propulsion through the birth canal arouses a determined aggressive response. During this process its psyche is also bombarded with a flood of erotic, destructive, demonic, scatological, and pyrocathartic imagery; this is acknowledged in the Vedic tradition which speaks of the 5,000 images which the fetus encounters during birth. Heavy transits of Pluto to Mercury can activate obsessive patterns of thought, rooted in these memories. The solution is to face the underlying BPM III material in responsible holotropic or psychedelic states.

Do I have Mercury-Pluto natally?

When did I have a Pluto-to-Mercury transit and what was my experience?

Some famous people who have it:

People in my life who have it:

Notes and Research

Notes and Research

Mercury-Uranus

Core Meanings   +

-

Loyalty to petrified opinion never yet broke a chain or freed a human soul.
   Mark Twain (Mercury square Uranus) Inscription beneath his bust
   in the Hall of Fame.

I tore myself away from the safe comfort of certainties through my love for truth; and
truth rewarded me.
   Simone de Beauvoir (Mercury conjunct Uranus) *All Said and Done*,
   1974

The mind is not sex-typed.
   Margaret Mead (Mercury conjunct Uranus) *Blackberry Winter*, 1972

Fig. 33 Art by Eva Ursiny.

Do I have Mercury-Uranus natally?

When did I have a Uranus-to-Mercury transit and what was my experience?

Some famous people who have it:

People in my life who have it:

Notes and Research

Fig. 34 Mark Twain (Mercury square Uranus)

Notes and Research

Class 9

Venus-Neptune

Core Meanings   +

-

How do I love thee? Let me count the ways.
I love thee to the depth and breadth and height
My soul can reach.
    Elizabeth Barrett Browning (Venus trine Neptune) *Sonnets from the Portuguese,*
    1850

By learning the language of heavenly patterns, we begin to see that everything is mar-
ried to everything.
    Caroline W. Casey (ME=VE/NE) *Making the Gods Work for You,* 1998

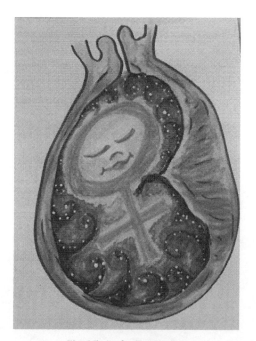

Fig. 35 Art by Eva Ursiny.

Do I have Venus-Neptune natally?

When did I have a Neptune-to-Venus transit and what was my experience?

Some famous people who have it:

People in my life who have it:

Notes and Research

Notes and Research

Venus-Saturn

Core Meanings +

-

Lots of people want to ride with you in the limo, but what you want is someone who will take the bus with you when the limo breaks down.
    Oprah Winfrey (Venus square Saturn)

Loneliness and the feeling of being unwanted is the most terrible poverty.
    Mother Teresa (Venus square Saturn-Moon) "Saints Among Us"

'Tis better to have loved and lost
Than never to have loved at all.
    Alfred Lord Tennyson (Venus quincunx Saturn) "In Memoriam" 1850

Figs. 36-37 Mother Teresa. Art on right by Eva Ursiny.

Do I have Venus-Saturn natally?

When did I have a Saturn-to-Venus transit and what was my experience?

Some famous people who have it:

People in my life who have it:

Notes and Research

Fig. 38 Relationship complications in the astrology of the future. Art by Samantha Marando.

Notes and Research

Class 10

Venus-Pluto

Core Meanings   +

-

Love opens the doors into everything, as far as I can see, including and perhaps most of all, the door into one's own secret, and often terrible and frightening, real self.

    May Sarton (Venus sextile Pluto) *Mrs. Stevens Hears the Mermaids Singing*, 1965

'Fair and foul are near of kin,
And fair needs foul,' I cried....
But Love has pitched his mansion in
The place of excrement
For nothing can be sole or whole
That has not been rent.

    William Butler Yeats (Venus conjunct Pluto) "Crazy Jane Talks With the Bishop"

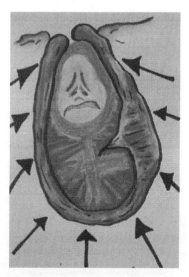

Fig. 39 Art by Eva Ursiny.

Do I have Venus-Pluto natally?

When did I have a Pluto-to-Venus transit and what was my experience?

Some famous people who have it:

People in my life who have it:

Notes and Research

Notes and Research

Venus-Uranus

Core Meanings   +

-

Each friend represents a world in us, a world possibly not born until they arrive, and it is only by this meeting that a new world is born.

    Anaïs Nin (Venus square Uranus) *The Diary of Anaïs Nin*, vol. 2, 1939-1949

A good marriage is one which allows for change and growth in the way they express their love.

    Pearl Buck (Venus square Uranus) *To My Daughters, With Love*, 1967

Figs. 40-41 Art on left by Eva Ursiny. Photo on right by Nicole Alexander.

Do I have Venus-Uranus natally?

When did I have a Uranus-to-Venus transit and what was my experience?

Some famous people who have it:

People in my life who have it:

Notes and Research

Fig. 42 "Peacock Great Mother Goddess" One of Grof's perinatal sessions in which he passed through the purifying fire of BPM III and into the blessed realm of rebirth and BPM IV. His transits at this time included Uranus-Pluto square his natal Venus. Art by Stan Grof.

Notes and Research

Class 11

Mars-Neptune

Core Meanings   +

-

Sexuality is a sacrament.
Starhawk (Mars trine Neptune) *The Spiral Dance: A Rebirth of the Ancient Religion of the Great Goddess,* 1979

There is no way to peace. Peace is the way.
Mohandas Gandhi (Mars quincunx Neptune)

 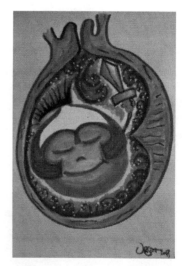

Figs. 43-44 Photo on left Mohandas Gandhi. On right: The amniotic Mars. Resembling existence in a cosmic womb, Neptune helps to soften, spiritualize, and hydrate Mars' dynamic energies, leading to a more relaxed, altruistic, and flowing approach to life. Mars can also encourage us to pursue, in more active and dynamic ways, Neptune's unitive states of being. Art by Eva Ursiny.

Do I have Mars-Neptune natally?

When did I have a Neptune-to-Mars transit and what was my experience?

Some famous people who have it:

People in my life who have it:

Notes and Research

Notes and Research

Mars-Saturn

Core Meanings   +

-

I have nothing to offer but blood, toil, tears, and sweat.
  Winston Churchill (Mars trine Saturn) First statement as British Prime
  Minister to the House of Commons, May 1940.

A small daily task, if it be really daily, will beat the labors of a spasmodic Hercules.
  Anthony Trollope (Mars conjunct Saturn) *An Autobiography*, 1883

If you hate a person, you hate something in him that is part of yourself. What isn't
part of ourselves doesn't disturb us.
  Hermann Hesse (Mars conjunct Saturn) *Demian*, 1919

Fig. 45 Mars-Saturn transits may sometimes feel like the no-exit stage of labor, in which the uterine walls are contracting around us, but the cervix is still closed and our energies have no easy outlet. We may feel stuck, frustrated, or blocked. Saturn presses in yet also focuses Mars' energy, in a firm tempering of the assertive and aggressive impulses. On the positive side, we can apply ourselves in steady and sustained ways during these periods, working long and hard to accomplish important goals and projects. Art by Eva Ursiny.

Do I have Mars-Saturn natally?

When did I have a Saturn-to-Mars transit and what was my experience?

Some famous people who have it:

People in my life who have it:

Notes and Research

Notes and Research

Class 12

Mars–Pluto

Core Meanings +

-

We cannot cure the evils of politics with politics. . . . Fifty years ago if we had gone the way of Freud (to study and tackle hostility within ourselves) instead of Marx, we might be closer to peace than we are.

   Anais Nin (Mars trine Pluto) Letter, 1974

To reach the port of heaven, we must sail sometimes with the wind and sometimes against it—but we must sail, and not drift, nor lie at anchor.

   Oliver Wendell Holmes (Mars trine Pluto) *The Autocrat of the Breakfast Table*, 1858

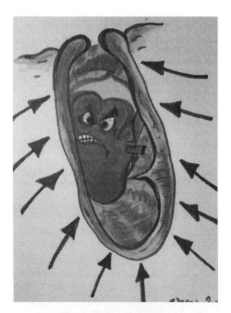

Fig. 46 Art by Eva Ursiny.

Do I have Mars-Pluto natally?

When did I have a Pluto-to-Mars transit and what was my experience?

Some famous people who have it:

People in my life who have it:

Notes and Research

Notes and Research

Mars-Uranus

Core Meanings   +

-

The only people for me are the mad ones, the ones who are mad to live, mad to talk, mad to be saved, desirous of everything at the same time, the ones who never yawn or say a commonplace thing, but burn, burn, burn, like fabulous yellow roman candles exploding like spiders across the stars and in the middle you see the blue centerlight pop and everybody goes "Awww!"

   Jack Kerouac (Mars square Uranus) *On the Road*, 1957

The only thing I regret about my past is the length of it. If I had to live my life over again I'd make all the same mistakes—only sooner.

   Tallulah Bankhead (Mars sextile Uranus)

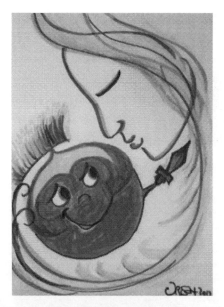

Fig. 47 Mars reborn. During transits of Mars-Uranus, you may enjoy exciting breakthroughs of energy, passion, and enthusiasm in many areas of your life. These are times when you can also resolve problems around anger and competition, by discharging the underlying aggressive energies in holotropic sessions. Art by Eva Ursiny.

Do I have Mars-Uranus natally?

When did I have a Uranus-to-Mars transit and what was my experience?

Some famous people who have it:

People in my life who have it:

Notes and Research

Notes and Research

Class 13

Jupiter-Neptune

Core Meanings   +

-

There are many paths up the mountain.
  Ramakrishna (Jupiter quincunx Neptune)

The Universe writes its metaphors in the most sweeping and majestic terms,
in the night's diamond sky, "deeper than day can comprehend."
  Richard Tarnas (Jupiter trine Neptune) *Prometheus the Awakener,* unpublished
  long version, 1980

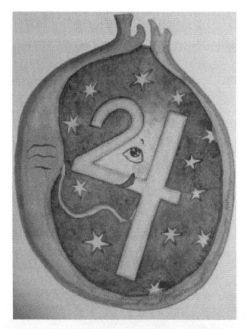

Fig. 48 The womb with a view, one of the blessed manifestations of Jupiter-Neptune. When people access memories of peaceful intrauterine life, they often enjoy a sense of spiritual oneness and life in heaven or paradise, what Grof calls the *melted* or *oceanic* type of ecstasy. The good womb experiences of BPM I include feelings of bliss and satiety on every imaginable level, including emotional and sexual satisfaction. Art by Olena Provencher.

Do I have Jupiter-Neptune natally?

When did I have a Neptune-to-Jupiter transit and what was my experience?

Some famous people who have it:

People in my life who have it:

Notes and Research

Fig. 49 The deeply committed civil rights leader and visionary, Martin Luther King, Jr., was born with a powerful grand trine of Jupiter-Saturn-Neptune.

Notes and Research

Jupiter-Saturn

Core Meanings   +

-

A mature person is one who does not think only in absolutes, who is able to be objective even when deeply stirred emotionally, who has learned that there is both good and bad in all people and in all things, and who walks humbly and deals charitably with the circumstances of life, knowing that in this world no one is all-knowing and therefore all of us need both love and charity.

    Eleanor Roosevelt (Jupiter sextile Saturn) *It Seems to Me*, 1954

Character cannot be developed in ease and quiet. Only through experience of trial and suffering can the soul be strengthened, vision cleared, ambition inspired, and success achieved.

    Helen Keller (Jupiter conjunct Saturn, with SA=JU/NE) *Helen Keller's Journal*, 1938

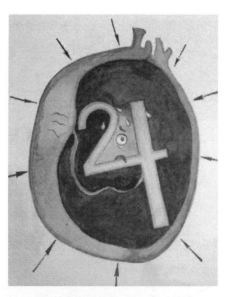

Fig. 50 Jupiter in the no-exit stage of labor (Grof's Basic Perinatal Matrix II). During Jupiter-Saturn transits, our sense of optimism and exuberance can feel blocked or curtailed. We might feel unfairly judged, dramatically unrecognized, or unable to advance. Saturnian reminders of our mortality can spur us to reevaluate our priorities in life. They help us to pursue satisfying experiences and quality connections with the people and nature around us, rather than striving blindly for compensations of inordinate wealth and position. As these archetypes resolve, we may also come to appreciate Saturn's focusing and sustaining effect, as we enjoy the rewards of systematic effort applied over long periods of time. Art by Olena Provencher.

Do I have Jupiter-Saturn natally?

When did I have a Saturn-to-Jupiter (or Jupiter-to-Saturn) transit and what was my experience?

Some famous people who have it:

People in my life who have it:

Notes and Research

Notes and Research

Class 14

Jupiter-Pluto

Core Meanings   +

-

The twentieth century's massive and radical breakdown of so many structures—cultural, philosophical, scientific, religious, moral, artistic, social, economic, political, atomic, ecological—all this suggests the necessary deconstruction prior to a new birth.
    Richard Tarnas (Jupiter opposition Pluto) *The Passion of the Western Mind*, 1991

Life, forever, dying to be born afresh, forever young and eager, will presently stand upon this earth as upon a footstool, and stretch out its realm amidst the stars.
    H. G. Wells (Jupiter trine Pluto) *The Outline of History*, 1920

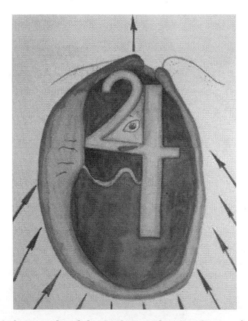

Fig. 51 The death-rebirth struggle of the Jupiter archetype. During these transits we may feel powerful evolutionary forces (Pluto) pressing on us to grow, evolve, and reach higher levels of integration (Jupiter) with the world around us. Jupiter helps to reveal the positive benefits in surrendering to Pluto's volcanic, cathartic forces in holotropic states. Art by Olena Provencher.

Do I have Jupiter-Pluto natally?

When did I have a Pluto-to-Jupiter transit and what was my experience?

Some famous people who have it:

People in my life who have it:

Notes and Research

Notes and Research

Jupiter-Uranus

Core Meanings +

-

Oh, the glory of growth, silent, mighty, persistent, inevitable! To awaken, to open up like a flower to the light of a fuller consciousness!
    Emily Carr (Jupiter-Uranus square Venus) *Hundreds and Thousands*, 1966

Let the winds of change blow through my life, bringing the most radically enlivening thing that could possibly happen. I am hoisting my sails.
    Caroline W. Casey (Jupiter sextile Uranus) *Making the Gods Work for You*, 1998

Fig. 52 Jupiter reborn. Like a grand replay of the miracle of birth, Jupiter-Uranus transits often coincide with exciting breakthroughs, expansion of horizons, and unexpected resolution of problems. The shadow of these archetypes is a kind of "golden touch" mania, as people develop a feeling that they are lucky or chosen beyond measure. These are natural and legitimate feelings for an ecstatic newborn. However, to reach the more peaceful and integrated states of BPM IV and rebirth, we might need to face any material in our psyches remaining from the death-rebirth struggle of BPM III. Art by Olena Provencher.

Do I have Jupiter-Uranus natally?

When did I have a Uranus-to-Jupiter (or Jupiter-to-Uranus) transit and what was my experience?

Some famous people who have it:

People in my life who have it:

Notes and Research

Fig. 53 Caroline W. Casey

Notes and Research

Class 15

Saturn-Neptune

Core Meanings   +

-

[Our] prenatal and perinatal history . . . has important implications for our spiritual life. As we have seen earlier, incarnation and birth represent separation and alienation from our true nature, which is Absolute Consciousness. Positive experiences in the womb and after birth are the closest contacts with the Divine that we can experience during our embryonal life or in infancy. The "good womb" and "good breast" thus represent experiential bridges to the transcendental level. Conversely, negative and painful experiences that we encounter in the intrauterine period, during birth, and in the early postnatal period send us deeper into the state of alienation from the divine source.

    Stanislav Grof (Saturn sesquiquadrate Neptune) *The Cosmic Game*, 1998

Where there is sorrow there is holy ground.

    Oscar Wilde (Saturn square Neptune) "De Profundis" 1905

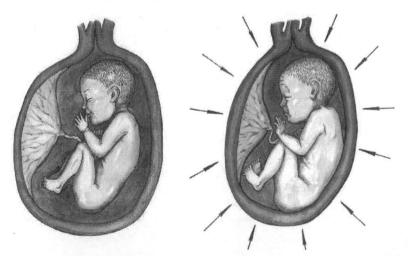

Figs. 54-55 The interplay of states of Neptunian unity and Saturnian separation in our lives can be very poignant. During these transits we may pass through periods in which our sense of peace, security, and connection has been interrupted or diminished. However, by facing our suffering honestly over time, we can work to gradually regain and sweeten the lost cosmic womb. We may then experience Saturn as a positive influence, helping us to be more humble, grounded, and disciplined in our spiritual practice. Art by Olena Provencher.

Do I have Saturn-Neptune natally?

When did I have a Neptune-to-Saturn (or Saturn-to-Neptune) transit and what was my experience?

Some famous people who have it:

People in my life who have it:

Notes and Research

Fig. 56 The new age finally comes to Antarctica. Art by Samantha Marando.

Notes and Research

Figs. 57-58 Saturn in BPM I and Neptune in BPM II. Resembling the fetus' loss of the womb paradise as the water breaks and the uterine walls contract around it, major Saturn-Neptune transits may coincide with a sense of wounded idealism, loss, or disorientation. It is important to face these feelings and let them register deeply. By allowing ourselves to feel our fear and cry, we make space for Neptune's divine grace to wash away the mortal sufferings of Saturn. Tears of sorrow become the blessed waters of life. Drawings by Jeremy Coyle.

Saturn-Pluto

Core Meanings   +

-

Saturn is seen as being an instrument in the service of the all-powerful Plutonic Deity, Shiva, the Great Destroyer and Creator. . . . In Shiva's feminine form, Pluto is Shakti, the Supreme Goddess, Mother Nature, the power and energy of the Universe, Kundalini; while Her destructive aspect is black Kali, the fierce devouring Mother. Thus, the Plutonic process of death and rebirth can be understood as an expression of Shiva's feminine aspect—the Divine Mother's birth process, the positive erotic Kundalini arousal, the destructive birth canal's contractions, Mother Nature's eternal regenerative power which bestows rebirth. Manifestations of Saturn-Pluto are her labor contractions, Jupiter-Pluto her birth orgasm.

> Richard Tarnas (SU=SA/PL) *Prometheus the Awakener*, unpublished long version, 1980

Long is the way
And hard, that out of hell leads up to light.

> John Milton (Saturn square Pluto) "Paradise Lost," 1667

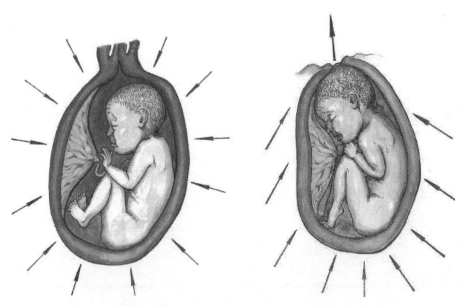

Figs. 59-60 Art by Eva Olena Provencher.

Do I have Saturn-Pluto natally?

When did I have a Pluto-to-Saturn (or Saturn-to-Pluto) transit and what was my experience?

Some famous people who have it:

People in my life who have it:

Notes and Research

Fig. 61 Drawing by Jeremy Coyle.

Notes and Research

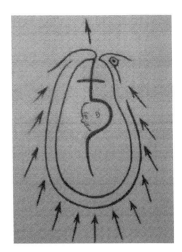

Fig. 62 Drawing by Jeremy Coyle.

Class 16

Saturn-Uranus

Core Meanings   +

-

The most radical revolutionary will become a conservative on the day after the revolution.
   Hannah Arendt (Saturn sextile Uranus) In *New Yorker*, 1970

The liberty of the individual must be thus far limited; he must not make himself a nuisance to other people.
   John Stuart Mill (Saturn conjunct Uranus) *On Liberty*, 1859

How glorious it is—and how painful also—to be an exception.
   Alfred de Musset (Saturn semisextile Uranus; with Jupiter opposition Uranus)
   La Merle Blanc, 1842

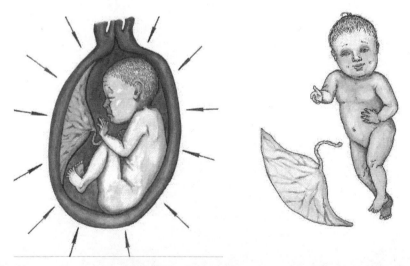

Figs. 63-64 The interplay of BPM II and BPM IV. During major Saturn-Uranus transits, our efforts toward freedom and change can sometimes feel delayed, blocked, or suppressed by Saturn. Some of these feelings are a replay of unresolved material from the no-exit stage of birth, Grof's BPM II. However, if we do systematic work to face and heal our past wounds, we may also gain access to the rebirth experiences of Uranus and BPM IV—as Saturn's persistence and staying power is then transformed into a positive influence. Art by Olena Provencher.

Do I have Saturn-Uranus natally?

When did I have a Uranus-to-Saturn (or Saturn-to-Uranus) transit and what was my experience?

Some famous people who have it:

People in my life who have it:

Notes and Research

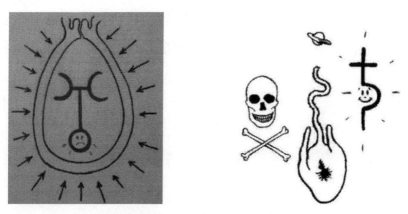

Figs. 65-66 Drawings by Jeremy Coyle.

Notes and Research

Fig. 67 The application of Promethean idealism.
Art by Eva Ursiny.

Neptune-Pluto

Core Meanings   +

-

The unconscious is not just evil by nature, it is also the source of the highest good: not only dark but also light, not only bestial, semihuman, and demonic but super-human, spiritual, and, in the classical sense of the word, "divine."
  C. G. Jung (MO=NE/PL) *The Practice of Psychotherapy*, 1953

We shall not cease from exploration
And the end of all our exploring
Will be to arrive where we started
And know the place for the first time.
  T. S. Eliot (Neptune conjunct Pluto) "Little Gidding," *Four Quartets*, 1942

God is a verb.
  Buckminster Fuller (Neptune conjunct Pluto) *No More Secondhand God*, 1963

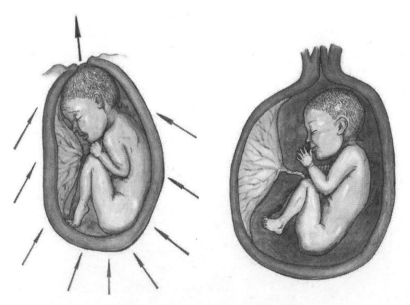

Figs. 68-69 Art by Olena Provencher.

Do I have Neptune-Pluto natally?

When did I have a Pluto-to-Neptune (or Neptune-to-Pluto) transit and what was my experience?

Some famous people who have it:

People in my life who have it:

Notes and Research

 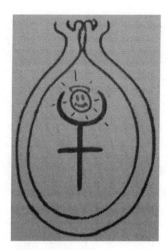

Figs. 70-71 Drawings by Jeremy Coyle.

Notes and Research

Class 17

Uranus-Pluto

Core Meanings   +

-

The rebellion against established structures of all kinds, the intense intellectual adventurousness and restlessness of the era, the radical consciousness transformation, the titanic technological advances in the space age, the general atmosphere of revolution on all fronts—all very much characteristic of the period 1960–72 when Uranus and Pluto were within 15° of exact conjunction.

   Richard Tarnas (Uranus semisquare Pluto) *Prometheus the Awakener*, 1995

The history of the world is none other than the progress of the consciousness of freedom.

   G. W. F. Hegel (Uranus trine Pluto) *Philosophy of History*, 1832

As long as you do not have it, this Die and Become, you are only a dreary guest on the dark earth.

   Johann von Goethe (PL=SU/UR)

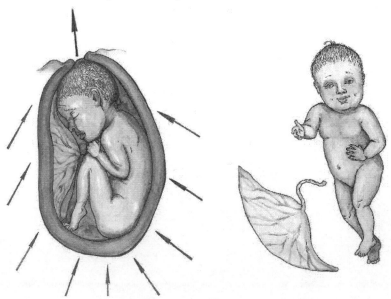

Figs. 72-73 Art by Olena Provencher.

Do I have Uranus-Pluto natally?

When did I have a Pluto-to-Uranus (or Uranus-to-Pluto) transit and what was my experience?

Some famous people who have it:

People in my life who have it:

Notes and Research

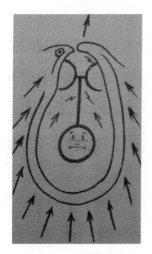

Figs. 74-75 Drawings by Jeremy Coyle.

Notes and Research

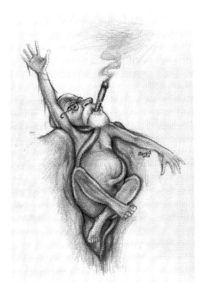

Fig. 76 Sigmund Freud, born with Sun-Uranus square Pluto. Art by Sergey Martyn.

Uranus-Neptune

Core Meanings   +

-

Uranus-Neptune's meaning implies . . . a radical shift or revolution of consciousness, involving the element of transcendence, compared to Uranus-Pluto's greater emphasis, as in the 1960's, on revolution with a more political and elemental component.

>   Richard Tarnas (NE=VE/UR) *Prometheus the Awakener*, long unpublished version, 1980

As if our birth had at first sundered things, and we had been thrust up through into nature like a wedge, and not till the wound heals and the scar disappears, do we begin to discover where we are, and that nature is one and continuous everywhere.

>   Henry David Thoreau (Uranus conjunct Neptune) *A Week on the Concord and Merrimack Rivers*, 1849

Figs. 77-78 Art by Olena Provencher.

Do I have Uranus-Neptune natally?

When did I have a Neptune-to-Uranus (or Uranus-to-Neptune) transit and what was my experience?

Some famous people who have it:

People in my life who have it:

Notes and Research

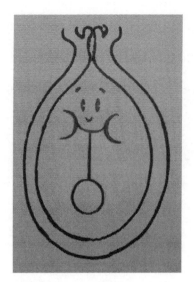

Fig. 79 Drawing by Jeremy Coyle.

Notes and Research

Fig. 80 Drawing by Jeremy Coyle.

Class 18

Sun-Moon

Core Meanings   +

-

The relationship of the Sun to the Moon can be understood if we regard the Sun as the basic energy of the self, while the Moon is the medium in which that energy operates. For example, the Sun is our basic will, our physical and psychological energy, representing our conscious intentions in life and our basic style of being and acting. The Moon represents the emotional context in which this process takes place, our sense of emotional security, unconscious attitudes, habits and psychological complexes built up during our earliest years.

   Robert Hand (Sun semisextile Moon) *Planets in Youth*, 1977

Every artist writes his own autobiography.

   Havelock Ellis (Sun conjunct Moon) *The New Spirit*

Do I have Sun-Moon natally?

When did I have a Sun-to-Moon transit and what was my experience?

Some famous people who have it:

People in my life who have it:

Notes and Research

Notes and Research

Sun-Mercury

Core Meanings   **+**

-

Knowledge, in truth, is the great sun in the firmament. Life and power are scattered with all its beams.
  Daniel Webster (Sun conjunct Mercury)

I think, therefore I am.
  Rene Descartes (PL=SU/ME) *Discourses on Method,* 1637

Do I have Sun-Mercury natally?

When did I have a Sun-to-Mercury (or Mercury-to-Sun) transit and what was my experience?

Some famous people who have it:

People in my life who have it:

Notes and Research

Notes and Research

Sun-Venus

Core Meanings +

-

Friendship with oneself is all-important, because without it one cannot be friends with anyone else in the world.
   Eleanor Roosevelt (Sun semisquare Venus) In *Ladies' Home Journal*, 1944

Instead of dirt and poison we have rather chosen to fill our hives with honey and wax; thus furnishing mankind with the two noblest of things, which are sweetness and light.
   Jonathan Swift (Sun conjunct Venus) *The Battle of the Books*, 1704

Do I have Sun-Venus natally?

When did I have a Sun-to-Venus (or Venus-to-Sun) transit and what was my experience?

Some famous people who have it:

People in my life who have it:

Notes and Research

Notes and Research

Sun-Mars

Core Meanings +

-

It is in vain to say human beings ought to be satisfied with tranquility: they must have action; and they will make it if they cannot find it.
    Charlotte Brontë (Sun sextile Mars) *Jane Eyre*, 1847

A talent is formed in stillness, a character in the world's torrent.
    Johann von Goethe (Sun trine Mars) *Torquato Tasso*, 1790

Fig. 81 Charlotte Brontë.

Do I have Sun-Mars natally?

When did I have a Mars-to-Sun (or Sun-to-Mars) transit and what was my experience?

Some famous people who have it:

People in my life who have it:

Notes and Research

Notes and Research

Class 19

Sun-Jupiter

Core Meanings   +

-

Oh, what a beautiful mornin'
Oh, what a beautiful day.
I got a beautiful feelin'
Everything's going my way.
    Oscar Hammerstein II (Sun conjunct Jupiter) "Oh, What a Beautiful Mornin,'"
    from *Oklahoma!*, 1943

For man, as for flower and beast and bird, the supreme triumph is to be most vividly, most perfectly alive.
    D. H. Lawrence (Sun conjunct Jupiter) *Apocalypse*, 1931

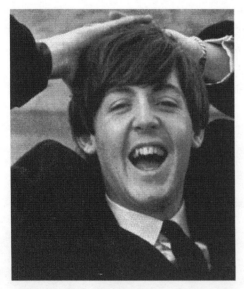

Fig. 82 Paul McCartney, born with Sun-Mercury-Jupiter square Neptune.

Do I have Sun-Jupiter natally?

When did I have a Jupiter-to-Sun transit and what was my experience?

Some famous people who have it:

People in my life who have it:

Notes and Research

Notes and Research

Moon-Mercury

Core Meanings   +

-

That is the happiest conversation where there is no competition, no vanity,
but a calm quiet interchange of sentiments.
   Samuel Johnson (Moon sextile Mercury) From James Boswell, *Life of Johnson*, 1791

There is only one thing in the world worse than being talked about, and that is not being talked about.
   Oscar Wilde (Moon square Mercury) *The Picture of Dorian Gray*, 1891

Fig. 83 Oscar Wilde.

Do I have Moon-Mercury natally?

When did I have a Mercury-to-Moon (or Moon-to-Mercury) transit and what was my experience?

Some famous people who have it:

People in my life who have it:

Notes and Research

Notes and Research

Moon-Venus

Core Meanings   +

-

Come live with me, and be my love;
And we will all the pleasures prove
That valleys, groves, hills, and fields,
Woods or steepy mountain yields.
  Christopher Marlowe (Moon-Uranus square Venus-Pluto)
  "The Passionate Shepherd to his Love" c. 1589

Happiness is a warm puppy.
  Charles M. Schulz (Moon square Venus-Sun)

Fig. 84 Christopher Marlowe.

Do I have Moon-Venus natally?

When did I have a Venus-to-Moon (or Moon-to-Venus) transit and what was my experience?

Some famous people who have it:

People in my life who have it:

Notes and Research

Notes and Research

Class 20

Moon-Mars

Core Meanings   +

-

Man is only truly great when he acts from the passions.
    Benjamin Disraeli (Moon conjunct Mars) *Coningsby*, 1844

I am woman, hear me roar.
    Helen Reddy (Moon square Mars) "I am Woman"

Fig. 85 Helen Reddy, photo by Francesco Scavullo.

Do I have Moon-Mars natally?

When did I have a Mars-to-Moon (or Moon-to-Mars) transit and what was my experience?

Some famous people who have it:

People in my life who have it:

Notes and Research

Notes and Research

Moon-Jupiter

Core Meanings   +

-

The more people have studied different methods of bringing up children the more they have come to the conclusion that what good mothers and fathers instinctively feel like doing for their babies is the best after all.

   Dr. Benjamin Spock (Moon trine Jupiter) *The Common Sense Book of Baby and Child Care*, 1946

A moral choice in its basic terms appears to be a choice that favors survival: a choice made in favor of life.

   Ursula K. Le Guin (Moon conjunct Jupiter) *Dancing at the Edge of the World*, 1989

Fig. 86 A book that changed the Western world.

Do I have Moon-Jupiter natally?

When did I have a Jupiter-to-Moon transit and what was my experience?

Some famous people who have it:

People in my life who have it:

Notes and Research

Notes and Research

Mercury-Venus

Core Meanings   +

-

Ideas themselves draw the human intelligence towards them with the force of Divine Eros, Ideas both in the sense of intellectual concepts and in the sense of archetypal Figures. One falls in love with a true Idea, is gripped by it with a passion, suffused by its meaning; the brain itself becomes an erogenous zone.
  Richard Tarnas (Mercury conjunct Venus)
  Prometheus the Awakener, unpublished long version, 1980

His laughter tinkled among the teacups.
  T. S. Eliot (Mercury conjunct Venus) "Mr. Apollinax" 1917

Do I have Mercury-Venus natally?

When did I have a Venus-to-Mercury (or Mercury-to-Venus) transit and what was my experience?

Some famous people who have it:

People in my life who have it:

Notes and Research

Notes and Research

Class 21

Mercury-Mars

Core Meanings   +

-

We are most likely to get angry and excited in our opposition to some idea when we ourselves are not quite certain of our own position, and are inwardly tempted to take the other side.

Thomas Mann (Mercury opposition Mars) *Buddenbrooks*, 1903

Our swords shall play the orators for us.

Christopher Marlowe (Mercury square Mars) *Tamburlaine the Great*

Do I have Mercury-Mars natally?

When did I have a Mars-to-Mercury (or Mercury-to-Mars) transit and what was my experience?

Some famous people who have it:

People in my life who have it:

Notes and Research

Notes and Research

Mercury-Jupiter

Core Meanings   +

-

And this gray spirit yearning in desire
To follow knowledge, like a sinking star
Beyond the utmost bound of human thought.
   Alfred Lord Tennyson (Mercury square Jupiter) "Ulysses" 1842

Training is everything. The peach was once a bitter almond; cauliflower is nothing but cabbage with a college education.
   Mark Twain (Mercury trine Jupiter) "Pudd'nhead Wilson," 1894

Fig. 87 Oprah Winfrey—actress, talk show host, media executive, television producer, and philanthropist—is one of the most positive, influential, and idealistic figures in the modern world. She was born with a grand trine of Mercury, Jupiter, and Neptune.

Do I have Mercury-Jupiter natally?

When did I have a Jupiter-to-Mercury (or Mercury-to-Jupiter) transit and what was my experience?

Some famous people who have it:

People in my life who have it:

Notes and Research

Notes and Research

Venus-Mars

Core Meanings   +

-

In astrology, the concepts of masculinity and femininity have nothing to do with men and women per se, but refer to the active and passive principles that operate throughout the cosmos. Every man and every woman is an amalgam of active and passive forces in varying degrees of tension and interplay, with the tension, or disequilibrium, providing the basis for human sexual motivation.
    John Townley (VE=MA/PL) *Planets in Love*, 1978

The words "Kiss Kiss Bang Bang" which I saw on an Italian movie poster, are perhaps the briefest statement imaginable of the basic appeal of movies.
    Pauline Kael (Venus sextile Mars) *Kiss Kiss Bang Bang*, 1968

Man is a social animal.
    Baruch Spinoza (Venus conjunct Mars) *Ethics*, 1677

Do I have Venus-Mars natally?

When did I have a Mars-to-Venus (or Venus-to-Mars) transit and what was my experience?

Some famous people who have it:

People in my life who have it:

Notes and Research

Notes and Research

Class 22

Venus-Jupiter

Core Meanings   +

-

To know of someone here and there whom we accord with, who is living on with us, even in silence—this makes our earthly ball a peopled garden.
    Johann von Goethe (Venus opposition Jupiter) *Wilhelm Meister's Apprenticeship*, 1796

A very merry, dancing, drinking,
Laughing, quaffing, and unthinking time.
    John Dryden (JU=VE/NE) "The Secular Masque" 1700

I didn't get dressed like this to go unnoticed.
    Liberace (Venus conjunct Jupiter) Attributed.

Fig. 88 Liberace, photo by Alan Light.

Do I have Venus-Jupiter natally?

When did I have a Jupiter-to-Venus (or Venus-to-Jupiter) transit and what was my experience?

Some famous people who have it:

People in my life who have it:

Notes and Research

Fig. 89 Actress Jennifer Lawrence was born with Venus conjunct Jupiter, in a wide opposition with Saturn.

Notes and Research

Fig. 90 Actress Scarlett Johansson was born with Venus conjunct Jupiter, in a triple conjunction with Neptune.

Mars-Jupiter

Core Meanings   +

-

One hour of life, crowded to the full with glorious action, and filled with noble risks, is worth whole years of those mean observances of paltry decorum.
  Walter Scott (Mars trine Jupiter) *Count Robert of Paris*, 1832

Latins are tenderly enthusiastic. In Brazil they throw flowers at you.
In Argentina they throw themselves.
  Marlene Dietrich (Mars conjunct Jupiter) In *Newsweek*, 1959

Fig. 91 Known as "Moses" by her admirers, American abolitionist and humanitarian Harriet Tubman was born with Mars square Jupiter-Neptune

Do I have Mars-Jupiter natally?

When did I have a Jupiter-to-Mars (or Mars-to-Jupiter) transit and what was my experience?

Some famous people who have it:

People in my life who have it:

Notes and Research

Notes and Research

Goodbyes

Additional Transits

Pluto-Pluto

Neptune-Neptune

Uranus-Uranus

Saturn-Saturn

Jupiter-Jupiter

Mars-Mars

Venus-Venus

Mercury-Mercury

Moon-Moon

Sun-Sun

VIII

The Cosmic Love Affair
(From *The Astrology of Love and Relationships*)

We are told by the mystics that existing beyond time and space—as well as every particle within it—is a field of self-observing consciousness, sometimes referred to as the *Macrocosmic Void, Universal Mind, Divine Consciousness, God,* or *Goddess.* Neptune is the astrological symbol for this field of eternal, self-observing awareness which underlies all forms in the universe. Before the physical universes were created, this primal awareness yearned for something outside of itself, which it could relate to, love, and appreciate. Because nothing existed beyond itself, it had to subdivide pieces of its own being into separate units of consciousness, which could then interact with the Universal Mind and with each other, in the countless dramas of material incarnation.

From out of its infinite nature it differentiated out essential principles—which have been referred to as gods and goddesses, first causes, Forms, or archetypes. The Universal Mind's impulses toward love became the archetype we call Venus; its nurture, the Moon; its energy, Mars. Every archetypal principle adds something essential to the physical cosmos. Saturn brings structure, boundaries, and solidity; Jupiter growth, expansion, and integration; Uranus change, awakening, and breakthrough. The archetypes further differentiate and blend into denser and denser layers of awareness, in order to create the material world of human beings, animals, plants, and matter.

Every part of the physical universe, from planets to atoms to human   beings, is ultimately the Universal Consciousness incarnated as that entity or thing. Some of the motives for the Universal Consciousness to incarnate itself as the material universe are described by the mystics as an overflowing love it wants to share with someone outside of itself, the creative passion of an artist, the boundless curiosity of a scientist, or, simply, cosmic boredom or even loneliness. The Universal or Divine Consciousness also seems to desire adventures that it could not have in the state of transcendence. These include our enjoyment of relationships, friendships, food, music, nature, sexuality, and other experiences. Divine Consciousness seems to crave the full range of experience that incarnated life can offer.

Thus, although we are essentially a split-off piece of the Divine field, while we are in the incarnated state, we experience suffering and fear of death. We yearn to transcend the separate state and reawaken to our lost wholeness. While the Divine needs us, we need the Divine, and this mutual appreciation and reunion is one of the most important goals of the spiritual quest.

Every human being is thus a piece of the Universal Consciousness incarnated into physical form. We are not human beings trying to have a spiritual experience; we are one spiritual Being having all the experiences. From this perspective, the highest benefit of sex is the discharge of biological tensions, in order to reach a blissful reunion with our true cosmic identity. The ecstasy in romantic encounters, whether feelings of physical pleasure, romantic love, tender union, or transcendent rapture, comes from the nearness of the Divine—from freeing our essential energies and accessing our higher nature, beyond the confines of the separate individual state. For people interested in exploring these insights more deeply, I recommend Grof's book *The Cosmic Game* (1998).

Birth and Awakening

As we have seen, the birth process is one of the critical thresholds where Divine Consciousness buries itself into physical form and temporarily hides its true identity. The fetus in a healthy womb enjoys an open, seamless union with the entire universe. As the uterine walls contract, its consciousness is compressed into the boundaries of its body. The hours of life-threatening suffering in the birth canal constrict the fetus' awareness, breaking the blissful connection with the mother and with Divine Consciousness. Its awareness becomes tied to the physical body, separate from the surrounding world—boundaried now in space, and because of the onset of mortality, also finite in time.

The birth process is where the Universal Consciousness becomes an individual consciousness, the spiritual is made physical, the Divine "is made flesh." Birth can be seen as a step-down transformer station where collective consciousness, energies, and karma can enter the world of time and space to be experienced, lived through, and resolved. Biological death represents, then, the full awakening of the Universal Consciousness out of the separate condition once more. However, we can access the state of spiritual wholeness beyond death, in holotropic and psychedelic states before we die. Ideally, our sexual experiences will also present opportunities to work through the wounding blocks in energy and emotion which prevent us from remembering our higher nature.

Looking at this from the side of the individual psyche, birth and death are important gateways back to states of spiritual union. The integration and processing of our birth and the facing of death are crucial thresholds in shedding the blinders of separate ego identity and reawakening to our deeper cosmic status. The main purpose of archetypal and holotropic astrology is to support us in undergoing this process, to help us reawaken to the eternal Universal Self within our beings.

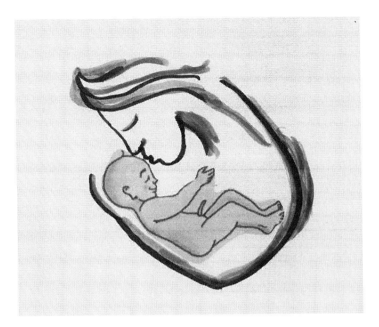

Fig. 92 BPM IV-Rebirth. Mother by Eva Ursiny, newborn by Stan Grof.

Glossary of Terms

Applying Transit When a transiting planet has not yet reached the point of exact transit to a natal planet and is moving toward it.

Archetype Patterns of experience and meaning. C. G. Jung coined this term to describe primordial patterns of experience and symbolism that emerge in the spiritual systems, mythology, and fairy tales of all cultures, as well as being spontaneously produced in people's dreams, fantasies, and inner lives. Some of the archetypes or eternal forms that Jung observed were the Anima and Animus, Shadow, Descent into the Underworld followed by Rebirth, Eternal Child, and the Self.

The fundamental insight of astrology, according to Richard Tarnas, is that there is a one-to-one correlation between archetypes and the planets in the solar system. Each planet corresponds to a major archetype or group of archetypes: Uranus to Rebirth and the Eternal Child, Pluto to the Descent into the Underworld and Evolution, Venus to Love and Beauty, and so forth. The interaction of planets in the birth chart creates a blend of archetypal meanings, like a series of personal myths. Astrology can illuminate the dominant archetypal patterns in an individual's life, and specifically *when* a given archetypal principle is likely to be activated.

Aspects Significant angular relationships between two or more planets that cause the archetypal qualities associated with those planets to interact and express their natures together.

Basic Perinatal Matrices (BPMs) Clusters of experience that occur when people explore the perinatal layer of their psyche. By extrapolating from a large amount of clinical data, Stanislav Grof observed that perinatal experiences—sequences of psychological death and rebirth—tend to occur in four distinct clusters or complexes. He termed these the *Basic Perinatal Matrices* or *BPMs* I-V. They are: I) *The Amniotic Universe,* II) *Cosmic Engulfment* or *Hell,* III) *The Death-Rebirth Struggle* or *Purgatory,* and IV) *Separation from the Mother* or *Rebirth.* Each perinatal matrix is based around a specific stage of labor, while at the same time having archetypal experiential components that far surpass the biological aspects of birth.

Tarnas discovered there was an exact thematic correlation between the experiences of individuals influenced by these matrices and the archetypal meanings associated with the planets Neptune, Saturn, Pluto, and Uranus.

Caesarean Birth The pattern in an *emergency* caesarean birth is essentially the same as with a vaginal delivery. The infant passes from the (often) blissful situation in the womb, to the extreme suffering of BPM II, then possibly to the agonizing struggle in the birth canal of BPM III, and then experiences rescue from the outside as they are surgically removed from the mother's body. The sequence passes from womb, to life-threatening birth canal, to breakthrough out into the world, in an ecstatic release of pressure. The moment of birth and situation in the delivery room are experienced as a dramatic liberation and improvement by the fetus, incomparably better than the life-threatening pressures in the birth canal.

Both a vaginal delivery and an emergency caesarean birth impart a deep sense that we can endure difficult situations and survive. We gain a natural template in our psyches for experiences of extreme pressure or suffering, which are then followed by release and breakthrough. Grof believe this is nature's way of creating optimism and tenacity in human beings, a deeply ingrained feeling that we can survive challenging situations and come out the other side. This endurance was absolutely necessary for our Stone Age ancestors to persevere in the often-difficult conditions of their lives.

Elective caesarean births, on the other hand, present a different sequence, with some advantages and disadvantages. The infant passes from the ecstatic situation of the womb directly into the delivery room, with its experiential polarities of hunger and thirst, dry and wet, heat and cold, and bright light. The world is experienced as significantly worse than the blissful womb. Sometimes elective caesarean-born people feel that they missed some fundamental pattern that is natural and necessary for human development. However, these feelings of omission can be worked through in sessions.

On the positive side, an elective caesarean baby will have less birth trauma, pain which can block access to the blissful memory of the womb and spiritual unity with the divine. They may have easier access to mystical and imaginative states, and even approach the world as if it were a great friendly womb. However, if people and events do not corroborate this expectation of safety and friendliness, they may become deeply hurt and withdraw back into themselves—lacking an innate sense of endurance and capacity to withstand adversity. See *A Different Doorway: Adventures of a Caesarean Born* by Jane English.
www.eheart.com/cesareanvoices/DD-revised.pdf

COEX Systems (Systems of Condensed Experience) Grof discovered that when powerful uncovering techniques were used, such as Grof® Breathwork or Holotropic Breathwork®, his clients relived sequences of experience connected by a common emotional theme or sensation. For example, a person involved in deep self-exploration might have a sequence of experiences related to shame, from the most recent back to deeper events, and finally to a core experience, which was often a facet of the birth process or an even deeper transpersonal root.

Other frequent examples of COEX themes include threads of memories involving failure, grief, or personal breakthrough, or experiences connected by a similar physical sensation such as choking or pressure in a certain part of the body.

Commission Problems of *commission* occur when a traumatic, especially a life-threatening, event has not been fully digested, and leaves a trace or residue in a person's psyche. A foreign, disorganizing experience has intruded into the person's psyche and being. These types of problems can be released by fully experiencing the original event and allowing its energies and emotions to be discharged and consume themselves.

Grof® Breathwork is the form of holotropic breathwork that Stan Grof wishes to be taught and practiced by the Grof® Legacy Training, founded by Stan and Brigitte Grof in 2020. The technique of holotropic breathwork was created by Stan and his late wife Christina in 1974 at the Esalen Institute in California, as a non-drug substitute for his clinical research in psychedelic-assisted psychotherapy. A powerful avenue for healing and self-exploration, the process uses deep and rapid breathing, evocative music, focused bodywork, and mandala drawing to access holotropic states of consciousness in a supportive group context.

In this approach, the psyche is recognized as containing a wide spectrum of material, including memories from infancy to the present, sequences of death and rebirth, transpersonal phenomena, and profound spiritual experiences. Facilitators are aware of and comfortable with the full range of possible experiences, and there is no priority placed on one experience over another. The participant controls the intensity of the session through their own breathing and can stop the process at any time. Facilitators are not viewed as technicians manipulating the psyche toward a certain predefined goal but as trained co-explorers, who provide a safe and encouraging context for each person to find their own answers at their own pace. The psyche's intrinsic healing mechanisms and inner healer are deeply supported and respected.

When occurring in a day-long format, participants usually meet the night before on Zoom or sometime previously to discuss the protocols and format of the session. The next day they gather in the morning and introduce themselves, then each person chooses a partner. One person "breathes" before lunch while the other acts as a sitter. Sitting involves keeping the participant safe while they surrender to their emerging inner material, reminding them to breathe deeply, and offering support if requested. A verbal contract is made before the session in which the breather makes explicit what kinds of intervention they want—and this is always honored.

The facilitators, who are ideally a male-female dyad, choose the music, check on people during the experience, make interventions when appropriate and asked for, and in the final stages offer focused bodywork to any unresolved participants. Afterward, each participant draws a mandala. After lunch the process is repeated. When everyone is back in normal consciousness there is an optional group sharing. The facilitators ensure that each person is in a relaxed and stable state of mind before leaving. Each session is complete in itself but is also part of an open-ended spiritual quest that can be pursued whenever a person feels the need to do some deep processing work.

Grof® Breathwork is compatible with other therapeutic techniques that involve deep self-exploration. It can be used as an adjunct to therapy, an activating technique for clients who are "stuck," or a backup modality for highly emotive clients or those experiencing spiritual emergency. It is also very beneficial for healthy and well-adjusted individuals who are looking for deeper answers and meaning in their lives. Finally, it is one of the most useful and comprehensive practices available for people who are training to become therapists and sitters in the field of psychedelic-assisted psychotherapy.

Holotropic A term coined by Grof, from *trepein* = "moving toward" and *holos* = "wholeness." The holotropic impulse is the impulse in our psyche—directed by our own "inner healer"—to shed our limited perceptions and experience our identity as being bigger than the boundaries of the ego, ultimately as being commensurate with the field of Universal Consciousness itself.

Holotropic states of consciousness offer a temporary opening to a range of experiences normally inaccessible to us in the everyday or *hylotropic* mode of consciousness. These include memories from childhood, sequences of dying or being (re)born, fetal experiences, ancestral memories, past lives, identification with other people or groups of people, the consciousness of animals or plants, experience of other dimensions, mythological terrains and sequences, archetypes, or identification with the Universal Mind, Absolute Consciousness, or the Macrocosmic Void.

Holotropic states, when entered into with proper supervision, have dramatic healing potential. They have been pursued in a systematic way by all or most non-Western and pre-industrial societies, often as a central part of the society's spiritual life. The variety of methods used to enter holotropic states include rites of passage, aboriginal healing rituals, fasting, meditation, trance dancing, breathing maneuvers, sensory deprivation or overload, and use of psychedelic substances.

Hylotropic From *trepein* = "moving toward" and *hylos* = "matter." Grof's term to describe the impulse in consciousness which keeps our attention focused on the everyday, here-and-now layer of reality. To be a realistic, functioning person we need to be able to operate in the hylotropic mode of consciousness. However, when this everyday, hylotropic mode of perception dominates our consciousness, it tends to result in a dry, barren, and meaningless way of experiencing the world—what Grof calls a "rush-hour, hamburger stand" mode of reality.

To find healing and deeper meaning in life we need to periodically enter into another type of consciousness—called *holotropic*—and integrate these experiences back into our everyday life. Grof gives the example that when we are landing a jet at O'Hara Airport, we want to be in the hylotropic mode of consciousness. To find perspective on our true authentic identity and role in the universe, we need to periodically enter the holotropic mode of consciousness.

An Integral or Spectrum Approach to Psychology Ken Wilber addresses the problem of why there are so many different psychological schools and paths of personal growth. He says that each school of psychology focuses on a different layer of the psyche, to the exclusion of the other layers—as they take the insights from one layer and attempt to extrapolate them to every other layer. The various competing theories are not so much right or wrong as they are accurate for the layers of the psyche they address, and not accurate for other layers.

Thus, Freud had essentially correct principles for the biographical layer of the psyche, but his theories are totally inadequate when addressing the spiritual dimensions of the unconscious. C. G. Jung focused on aspects of the transpersonal layer but did not integrate the powerfully energetic and cathartic experiences of the perinatal layer. A person's problems can only be resolved by addressing the specific layer of the psyche where they originate. For example, a person cannot resolve a memory of near-death through choking in the birth canal by talking about sibling rivalry or their oppressive father.

In his excellent article, "Holotropic Practice and the Promise of Full-Spectrum Transformation" (2014), Martin Boroson writes that: "Each form of therapy or spiritual practice has its own list of proscribed behaviors and recommended techniques. For example, in Zen meditation, the instruction might be to sit absolutely still, in order to avoid distraction, but in tantra, the instruction might be to follow every desire until one experiences ecstasy. In bioenergetic therapy, one might be encouraged to punch a cushion to give full expression to one's anger, but in kundalini yoga, the instruction might be to keep anger internal and channel this energy toward enlightenment."

Boroson notes that Grofian approaches to breathwork function by activating an intrinsic inner radar that zeroes in on the most relevant material for that individual, at that moment in time. It offers a technique for full experience of whatever *the psyche itself* selects as important, including various experiences along the full spectrum of the human psyche. Some sessions would have the character of a bioenergetics session, others like a Jungian exploration of archetypes, and still others like a shamanic rite of passage. He considers Grof's approach to breathwork a prime example of an integral path.

Intrinsic Human Values   Grof consistently observed these positive human characteristics that arise automatically when a person has worked through the traumatic leftover material from their psyches, especially the life-threatening passage through the birth canal. These include a high value placed on warm relationships, appreciation of nature, urge to do meaningful work, and cooperation to find solutions to shared social and ecological problems. Individuals in touch with these default layers of human nature and the universe see the exaggerated striving for power, money, or prestige as an immature compensation against the unconscious fear of dying and memory of birth. They also feel critical attitudes toward the abuse of power.

Kundalini   An electrifying energy that arises in people's consciousness who are pursuing concentrated spiritual practices, and sometimes spontaneously. Kundalini awakening is like a supercharged evolutionary force cleaning out the blocks and unconscious areas in a person's body and psyche. It is important to have access to deep processing in supervised holotropic or psychedelic states, in order to keep up with and integrate the emerging material.

Midpoints The strongest type of midpoint is when a planet sits midway between two other planets. This combines the archetypal energies of the three planets, similar to a weak conjunction.

Natal "Birth." Natal planets are the positions the planets were in at the moment of our first independent breath.

Omission Problems in the psyche caused by unfulfilled valid needs for touch, cuddling, and rocking in early infancy. Omission problems leave a kind of vacuum in the psyche, which creates a feeling of emotional starvation in adult life—a person may spend their entire life looking for the love they missed as an infant or child. Grof observed that these vacuums can only be filled by regressing to the original state of emotional vulnerability and then receiving the appropriate nurture from a therapist, guide, or sitter. This process is similar to the psychological techniques known as "reparenting" and "corrective emotional experiences." This kind of physical contact should be available but only offered when requested by the journeyer themselves, and conducted with peer supervision.

Orbs The allowable number of degrees from exact, in which we consider two planets to be interacting, by aspect or transit. See the graphic on p. 15.

Perinatal *Peri* = surrounding and *natal* = birth. Grof applied this term to describe the layer of the unconscious psyche which contains experiences of birth and death, with the two always intermixed so that dying to the old becomes birth into the new. Perinatal experiences appear with verifiable details from actual childbirth alternating with sociological, archetypal, and karmic elements which have the same experiential flavor. These experiences tend to occur in four distinct clusters or complexes, which Grof refers to as the Basic Perinatal Matrices or BPMs.

   The perinatal layer of the psyche is in between and forms a bridge between the biographical layer of the psyche (events from the lifetime) and the transpersonal layers (experiences that transcend individual consciousness). The perinatal layer—birth and death—represents the boundaries of individual human existence. From a higher perspective, perinatal experiences can be seen as a kind of transformer station where collective energies, archetypes, and karma enter an individual human incarnation.

Separating Transit When a transiting planet has passed the point of exact transit to a natal planet and is moving away from it.

Spiritual Emergency A term coined by Stan and Christina Grof to describe periods of dramatic psychospiritual opening. These states can occur as a result of concentrated spiritual practice, or sometimes spontaneously. Spiritual emergency or emergence states require commitment from the experiencer and knowledgeable support from others to resolve. If supported and allowed to complete themselves, these states can result in major inner healing and transformation. See their books *The Stormy Search for the Self* and *Spiritual Emergency* (as coeditors).

Synchronicity An "acausal connecting principle" which was studied and documented by Swiss psychiatrist C. G. Jung. Synchronicity occurs when two events are meaningfully connected without one causing the other, for example thinking about someone just before they call. Because planetary alignments do not "cause" human experiences, the entire field of astrology is based on synchronicities. The integration of Jung's work, through figures such as Dane Rudhyar, Liz Greene, and Robert Hand, effected a dramatic quantum leap in the evolution of astrology. I believe an equally important development is now occurring with the integration of Grof's expanded cartography of the human psyche.

Transcendence Experiences of our true identity as being bigger and more inclusive than the limited ego-body identification—going beyond what Alan Watts called "the skin-encapsulated ego." Transcendent experiences represent partial or total access to realms beyond the limits of human birth and death. They are one of the prime goals of spirituality and recognized as having a "meta-healing" value in transpersonal forms of psychotherapy. Transcendent experiences bring an ecstatic freeing of consciousness from the fear of biological death and dying, renewed zest for life, meaningful connection with other people, nature, and cosmos, and an opening of creative channels.

Transits The interaction between a planet in the sky now with a planet's position at birth.

Transpersonal A term coined by Stanislav Grof in 1968 to describe states of consciousness that transcend the boundaries usually considered absolute in everyday reality. Transpersonal experiences occur in several broad forms: transcendence of space (such as identification with other people or groups of people), contraction of space (such as tissue, organ, cellular, DNA, molecular, or atomic consciousness), transcendence of time (ancestral, racial, or collective memories, phylogenetic memories, and past life experiences), or experiences beyond the time-space continuum as we know it altogether (archetypal personages and principles, mythological terrains and sequences, the Universal Mind, Absolute Consciousness, or the Supra-cosmic Void).

Transpersonal Psychology The branch of psychology and psychotherapy that seeks to integrate the spiritual dimensions of human nature into therapeutic practice. Transpersonal psychology acknowledges the complete spectrum of the human psyche, from the wounds and traumas of birth and early life, to spiritual realms of being that have a meta-healing value. A metaphor Grof uses is that verbal approaches to psychotherapy, with their biographical focus, can be compared with trying to ladle water out of a swamp, one spoonful at a time. Opening to the intrinsic spiritual dimensions of the psyche in experiential sessions, on the other hand, is like digging a trench from the swamp to the ocean, and allowing the cleansing ocean to flow in.

Transpersonal psychology was initiated in 1968 by Abraham Maslow, Stanislav Grof, Anthony Sutich, and others and is considered the "fourth wave" in psychology, after psychoanalysis, behaviorism, and humanism. Although predating the term, Carl Gustav Jung is considered the first transpersonally oriented psychiatrist of the modern era, for his articulation of the archetypes of the collective unconscious.

Acknowledgments

I am grateful to the students in my previous classes who suggested that a weekly balance of routine structure and specialized exploration would be the best combination. These include Tatiana Hassan, Alex Taylor, Marci Segal, and Lisa Leombruni. Many thanks and appreciations also to the students and colleagues who volunteered to read sections of the manuscript: Anne Marie Knop, Emily Wells, Ingrid Murphy, Jennifer Taylor, and Tanya Korpi.

I feel much gratitude for the hugely talented artists who helped to cocreate my perinatal illustrations and cartoons: Olena Provencher (Facebook page *Art of the Psyche*), Eva Ursiny (evaursiny.com), Samantha Marando (okeydokeydesign.com), Sergey Martyn, Myrto Papadaki, Jeremy Coyle, Elena Andrade, and Mango Johnstone. Deep appreciation also to the artists and colleagues who shared their evocative artistic creations. These include Stan Grof (grof-legacy-training.com), Silvina Heath, and Tauno Leinonen. Finally, a heartfelt thank you to my friend and colleague, Richard Tarnas, for his years of patient teaching and extensive research which determined the expanded orbs, multileveled and multivalent expressions, and correlations with Grof's discoveries which gave birth to this exciting new discipline.

Made in the USA
Monee, IL
20 May 2023

34156337R00164